I met Susan Woodward when she was a ranger at Petrified Forest and was immediately fascinated by her story. To have made such a radical life-change in the wake of a cancer diagnosis was not just brave, but completely inspiring. I have longed to understand the whole story from start to now, and this book lays out her journey in a way that is both humble and motivational. Reading her book made me want to recommit to the dream of roaming this great land in a wheeled house. This is a must-read for anyone contemplating the same path. – **Janice Holly Booth,** *Only Pack What You Can Carry* (National Geographic)

TURNING POINTS

How to Wake Up, Tune into Your GPS, and Get Unstuck

SUSAN C. WOODWARD

Printed in the United States of America
Published by Author Academy Elite
PO Box 43, Powell, OH 43065
www.AuthorAcademyElite.com

Library of Congress Control Number: 2020914154
- Paperback: 978-1-64746-410-3
- Hardback: 978-1-64746-411-0
- Ebook: 978-1-64746-412-7

Available in paperback, hardback, e-book, and audiobook
Some names and identifying details have been changed to
protect the privacy of individuals.

DEDICATION

For my great-aunt, Anita Tarbell
And for "Hickey" Harriet Clarke
Thank you both for seven glorious summers
at the Half-Moon Ranch.
Remembering you continues to inspire me.

Contents

A Note To The Reader

This book was going to be about my almost five years of full-time RVing, traveling throughout North America with my cat Bijou. I figured the writing was pretty much done since I had kept an ongoing journal of my travels; it would just need some tweaking here and there. I was wrong. As I wrote, I began to understand how much of who I was, and the choices I made were informed by the times in which I grew up and my childhood experiences.

My early and most important role models were my great aunt, Anita Tarbell, and a woman who worked with her, Harriet Clarke. Both were from the Boston area and educated as physical education instructors. In the 1920s, when Anita was in her late 20s, she went west for the summer to work on a dude ranch just north of Jackson Hole, Wyoming. The spread was homesteaded by an alcoholic cowboy and his Wellesley College-educated wife. Anita became partners with them and eventually bought them out. Hickey (Harriet's nickname) was head of the Physical Education Department at Radcliffe and started spending her summers working for Anita, leading pack-trips into the Teton Wilderness.

From age seven to age fourteen, I spent summers on the Half Moon Ranch, with about two dozen girls and half that number of boys, all from wealthy families on the East coast and the Buffalo area. Anita had connections in those areas through her years teaching physical education at various private girls' schools.

Hickey and Aunt Nita, as well as the other wonderful women who were in charge of us, taught us how strong and capable we were and instilled in me a deep love and respect for nature. We each had a horse, as well as saddle and tack, assigned to us for the summer. We rode every day, sometimes twice a day. We brushed and curried, saddled and unsaddled our horses and saddle-soaped the saddle and tack when needed. On the pack trips, which were terrific adventures and the highlight of the summers, we helped load up the panniers and pack the horses; we set up our tents, took care of our gear, dug latrines, washed and scrubbed dishes with sand and moss in the creeks or lakes, and helped Hickey with meal preparation. We weren't taken care of; we were responsible for ourselves and our gear. I don't recall any lectures. They taught us by modeling a different way of life.

In my 50s, I got curious about Anita and wanted to write a book about her. Yet, I knew nothing about so much of her life. What had ever possessed her to head for the west? And, in the 1920s, it was the *wild west*. I tried to track down Hickey and others who might have known her, but I'd waited too long. Aunt Nita had died, as had most of those who worked with her. The only contact still above ground was Grant Beck, who had a ranch in Pinedale. He had been the head cowboy during my seven summers. When I reached Grant, he told me Aunt Nita had gone with me on the pack trip my first year at the ranch. One evening, after I'd gone to bed, she and Grant had been talking by the campfire, and she told him she had been left at the altar. That was a surprise! My parents had never heard that; my grandmother, her sister, was dead so I couldn't ask her. But in the 1920s, it was likely considered an embarrassment, and no one would have talked about it. It could be she made up a story—who knows? But it could be that it took something like that to propel her into her Wild West adventure.

I married in 1965; the marriage ended ten years later when our boys were seven and nine. We had just bought a house in Harvard, Massachusetts. We sold it, and I had a smaller home built for the three of us. I worked at an insurance agency in town for several years, then became a Realtor. Thirteen years later, when the boys were grown and off on their own, I sold that house and moved with my cat Motor to North Carolina, where I started my real estate career all over again in Raleigh.

Now I was into my 60s, and the stars were aligning to launch me into an extraordinary adventure.

These days, most of us are familiar with GPS (Global Positioning System), a radio navigation system owned by the United States government, and operated by the United States Air Force. It uses satellite signals to tell you where you are in the physical world and how to get to where you want to be, driving a car. Things like dense clouds, or mountains, can interfere with the signal.

I have never wanted or felt I needed a GPS. We all have an internal GPS, though we've gotten out of the habit of using it, especially now that the government version seems to be standard in most newer cars. When we tune into our internal GPS, we intuitively receive guidance on making decisions for how to navigate our lives. At one period in my life, mine gave me a clear understanding, through dreams, of a situation I was dealing with. I could then usually see what steps to take. Now it happens more like a feeling in my heart or my gut that I'm making the right, or wrong, decision. And, unfortunately, I'm so accustomed to living in my head that I often totally miss what it is trying to tell me. Old habits or beliefs can mess with what your heart or gut is telling you. As with most skills, you need to practice.

Change can be a constant in every part of our lives: our job, our relationship, our finances. We must learn not to fear it, rather to embrace it, encourage and drive it.
— Tony Hsieh, CEO, Zappos Inc.

Part I

DESIGN YOUR NEW LIFE (2007-2008)

••• | •••

Cancer? No Thanks!

*Life is like riding a bicycle. To keep your balance
you must keep moving.* —Albert Einstein

IT WAS THE end of January 2004, and I had just closed on
the third home I'd bought as a single woman. I aimed for a
move-in date in mid-March. My mind was spinning, full of
questions about colors, furniture arrangement, things to do,
real estate sales to track, painting, packing. Should I sell or
rent the townhome? Was that a lump in my left breast?

I didn't have time to worry about that, so put it out of my
mind. But two weeks later, I felt it again and decided to get
it checked. It was a good thing I did since it turned out to be
cancer. My breath stopped, and my eyes filled with tears at
the news. "Early-stage, very treatable," said the surgeon.

Cancer must be one of the scariest words in the English
language. My mother's best friend died of breast cancer when
I was about ten, and I remembered that time well. So now

my mind started running horrible scenarios, usually in the middle of the night. During the days, I kept myself so busy there wasn't time to be scared. On March 8th, I underwent a lumpectomy. A week later, I moved into my new home, just a few days shy of my 62nd birthday.

I had some fears about the radiation treatment and, had I known more at the time, I might have refused it. The oncologist wanted me to do chemo as well, and to take a pill called anastrozole for five years. Those I turned down, partly because real estate was so busy at that time and I couldn't afford either the time or money for chemo. Also, I had a decided bias against pills. Mainly, I tried to distance myself from the whole idea of cancer. I worked hard and started to write more.

A month or so after the lumpectomy, seven-and-a-half weeks of radiation therapy began. How quickly life can change. How did this happen? I ate well, took care of myself, and generally felt I would live to be 120. But I enjoyed a big bowl of ice cream before bed each night, which resulted in several extra pounds of that toxic belly fat. My mother had died a year previously. A love affair with the man I'd been engaged to 36 years before had ended abruptly, and it had been two years since I'd put my cat Motor to sleep, so my life was lacking laughter. I stressed about things I believed were in my control when, of course, they were not. One of my friends suggested anger management classes. What? Me, angry? Hmmm.

Well, though I didn't like to admit it, I did have some anger issues. My mother and I had had a tense relationship at times. She had never taken care of her health, and I felt her doctors were enablers, giving her pills for this or that. She had an automobile accident several years before her death, and she hadn't made much effort to regain her strength and independence, so my dad ended up being a full-time caretaker. I saw the toll it took on him and worried about them both. I also felt terrible that she had died alone in the hospital. Dad had visited her a couple of days earlier, I'd been up for an extended visit over the holidays, but she died alone. And I was sad and hurt, and maybe angry that Dad had remarried six months after her death. It felt like I'd lost him too.

Thirty-six years ago, I was engaged to be married. Two weeks before the invitations went out, my fiancé called to say he couldn't go through with it. After almost three years of being his girl, I suddenly lost my identity. Who would I be now? There was a horrible feeling that, if I looked in the mirror, there would be no reflection. It frightened me, but I stuffed my shock and grief vowing I would never let myself be defined by a relationship again. Somewhere in my heart, a door slammed shut, though I didn't realize it at the time. Why did I ever let myself fall for him all over again? When he suddenly ended it this time, I grieved for both endings and wallowed in that shattered feeling for several days.

But you know, if you hang out in sadness and grief, nothing gets done. So, I pushed the feelings down. I'd gotten good at ignoring and stuffing uncomfortable emotions, but they don't go away. They fester somewhere in your body and bubble out in other ways—irritability, impatience, cancer, anger. I found that anger works for getting things done and for moving forward with your life.

As a coping strategy, refusing to feel your feelings may work in the short term, but my subsequent relationships likely paid the price.

It was spring. Buyers were keeping me busy, but whenever possible, I'd sit out on my screen porch and write, or think, or both. During those quiet times, I'd hear a little voice in my head. *You know all those things you want to do with your life? Maybe you should stop putting them off*, it cautioned.

5

I started to realize how little thought I had ever given to what kind of life I wanted to have. When I was in high school, nurse, teacher, or stewardess were the career choices mentioned most often for women. I was already too tall to be a stewardess and wasn't particularly interested in the other options. The default for a woman at that time was marriage and children, and I didn't spend much time imagining other lives.

I think I'm still working on figuring out who I am. Women's Lib started in the late 1960s when I was busy with a couple of toddlers. It confused a lot of people; I know it confused me. I've been divorced twice and have spent most of my life as a single woman. Women's Lib surely had something to do with it. And, come to think of it, Aunt Nita and Hickey were both single, strong, liberated women.

Bad things happen to everyone. We all face challenges; we all struggle at times. But we all get to choose the story we tell ourselves about whatever happens. I realized I was at a turning point, and I started asking myself the questions I should have asked several decades ago: What things were in my control, and did I want to change them? If so, how? How did I want to live my life? What did I love most about my life, and how could I create more of that? I loved animals—they had always been a part of my life, and I really missed Motor. So my first step was to acquire a sweet Russian Blue kitten. I named her Bijou.

Over the next couple of years, the real estate market was booming in Raleigh. I had started my own company a few years before and now had eight other agents. Business kept me hopping, but more and more that little voice claimed my attention. Was retirement or semi-retirement even possible?

Off and on throughout my life, I had enjoyed painting and writing. During my two years at Colby College, I'd taken art history and one or two drawing courses. I'd gone back to school part-time after moving to Raleigh, hoping to finish my art degree. I didn't quite make it, but in the past couple of years, finally making a decent income, I'd taken time out for art workshops. I wanted more time to paint, to travel, to read and write. Life seemed to be getting busier and more expensive. There had to be some way to reverse that trend, to opt-out of the busyness. Instead of being a human *doing*, was there a way to become a human *being*?

One morning, a program on National Public Radio caught my attention. NPR was interviewing people who lived part-time or full-time in an RV. Some were retired, and some were wealthy, but many found that the income-generating part of their life was transportable. The program was well-done, and it stuck in my memory.

I went to the local Winnebago dealer and spent time talking with them and watching a man and his wife hook up their new 5th Wheel trailer. There was no way I'd be able to do that by myself. That left Class A and Class C RVs, and 27-feet looked like it would work fine size-wise. There were many nights I woke up about two and couldn't get back to sleep, wondering if I could manage to drive a 27-foot RV while towing a car. It was too much to expect all the roads would be straight. There were no RV driver training schools in North Carolina. How did you hook up a car to a towbar?

Even a used RV was expensive. How could I make this work? The answer was obvious. Sell my house and all my belongings and live full-time in the RV with Bijou. Of course! I got excited and couldn't wait to start my new life.

I sent information and photos of some antiques, paintings, and jewelry to an auction house in Massachusetts I had dealt with before. I posted other items on Craigslist.

It soon became apparent that getting rid of all my belongings would be a lengthy process. It also occurred to me to wonder what I would do if I sold my house and then discovered that I couldn't stand living in an RV full-time. It would be better to hang onto the house for a while. I could travel for a few months in the winter, then come back in the early spring and play realtor again. That would give me a chance to save more and work at reducing my living expenses as well.

In the meantime, I ordered several books on RVing through inter-library loan and started reading up on this lifestyle.

In the course of my reading, I discovered that the vehicle you tow (the dinghy) should be standard shift if you want to tow it the safest way, with all four wheels on the ground. My almost-new RAV-4 was an automatic. I took it back and traded it in for a Toyota Corolla. The RAV-4 was a leased vehicle, and I'd had it for only six months, so there was a penalty for turning it in. But I cut my car payment in half and had better gas mileage, so would be even in a little over a year.

A few of my friends, on hearing of my plan, asked what I would do for money when I was traveling the country in my RV. It didn't even occur to me to worry about that. Long ago, when I was raising the boys, I'd worked various secretarial jobs through a temp agency, so I figured I could do that again. A couple of the RV books gave lots of guidance for finding work on the road, including gigs at national parks. Little by little, I envisioned a new life, one that gave me the time and space for writing and painting.

Next, I started reading books on retirement. The first few made me angry or depressed, as they concentrated on how much money you needed to amass before you could retire. Their main message was to start saving early, so it was already too late for me. Furthermore, if you managed to save a few hundred thousand, you then had to spend most of your time making sure you didn't lose it, moving it from place to place, and re-balancing your investments. That didn't sound like fun.

There was some money in an IRA and equity in my home. If I could hang in there another couple of years, both should grow, but they wouldn't produce much income with which to augment social security. The best course of action seemed to be to reduce my cost of living. So, I concentrated on that and taking care of my health.

My health was good. The possibility of a recurrence of cancer didn't worry me too much, but it's not easy to forget about the Big C. Twice a year, I went for a checkup and mammogram and held my breath until I got the all-clear signal. And there were frequent reminders of what could be lying in wait for me as well-known people became newsworthy for being diagnosed with breast, bone, or colon cancer. My lovely neighbor, Anne, had had breast cancer in one breast and, despite radiation and chemo, got cancer in the other nine years later and now had cancer in her bones.

Soon it was 2007. There was internal pressure to move forward with my dream, and I decided that this was going to be the year. I stopped by the Winnebago dealer in the early spring and asked the manager to please notify me if a good used one came in. I would buy it and worry about how to pay for it later. I believed the money would show up when I needed it.

I made mental lists of things I must remember to take with me when I finally drove off and started practicing water conservation when hand-washing dishes. Was my driveway wide enough for an RV? Every time I walked through the house, I saw more items to eliminate. I looked for other ways to make extra money. Lottery tickets?

A few books had great information about the best cities for retirees, based on the cost of living, job possibilities, and ideas for volunteering. Though these books didn't stress how much money you might need and how to manage it, they offered excellent advice about taking a hard look at your life situation. I was lucky in many ways. My parents had planned well, so there was little chance that my three brothers and I would need to help them financially. My boys were adults and on their own. I wasn't responsible for anyone but myself, and Bijou, of course.

One book, in particular, was most encouraging and had a long chapter about living in an RV, noting many places you could boondock (no water, sewer, or electric hookups) at little or no cost. It was clear that my plan was doable.

What all the great minds tell you is accurate: when you put your thoughts on a problem and start looking hard for solutions, the Universe moves to help you out.

First, the tenant in my townhome agreed to move out. He still owes me almost $3000 in back rent. As soon as he was out, I started in on cleaning up the mess he left behind. I installed new carpet, touched up paint, got general repairs done, planted a for-sale-by-owner sign in the yard, and put a few ads on the internet.

Amid all this activity, I received an invitation to attend an evening workshop regarding an internet marketing business opportunity. I had received these before and even wasted money on one of them about ten years previously. But, since I was looking for ways to make my dreams come true, I decided to check this one out.

I went to the workshop and signed up for an all-day seminar a couple of weeks later. I was sure I'd learn a lot that would be useful, and equally sure that I would not invest the several thousand dollars required to buy into their opportunity.

The all-day event was fantastic. I started to see real possibilities. Yes, I did invest in their opportunity. I felt that building a business online could be fun and could spell the difference between continually cutting corners and having the time and money to do the things I wanted to do.

The townhome sold quickly. The day before closing, I looked online at the RV dealer's site, and there was a used 27-foot Class A motorhome on the lot that looked good and was less money than I'd expected to spend. So, after the closing, I drove over to check it out.

The RV, a Winnebago Sightseer, was beautiful and seemed to be in excellent condition. I spent some time with the manager, asking questions, and getting his promise to teach me to drive it, then went home to think it over and do some research. By Monday morning, I knew I was ready to take the plunge, so I called him up and made an offer. An hour later, my offer was accepted.

My first driving lesson had me dry-mouthed, but he gave me high marks. The big test was going over speed bumps in his lot. He kept saying, "Slower, slower!" I was only going two or three miles an hour, but the RV wallowed like a big boat in a heavy swell. "You would have broken all your dishes there," he said.

I had to arrange financing and insurance, and the bills added up fast. If there were any more motivation needed to get my internet business going, I sure had it now.

Three years of planning and soul-searching had given me clarity. I still didn't know exactly how it would work but trusted that, somehow, it would. I was willing to do my part, and confident the Universe would take care of the details. There had always been a piece of me that wanted to be like Aunt Nita and Hickey. Like the two of them, almost 100 years ago, I was going to head West and see what happened.

I'd never had GPS in my car and had no plans for it in my RV. I don't totally trust computer software, preferring to rely on maps and my internal GPS. If I plan a route using a map, I have a picture in my mind of where I'm heading, and I like that a whole lot better than having an electronic voice continually telling me where I am and where to go next.

··· 2 ···

Freedom

Life isn't about finding yourself. Life is about creating yourself. — George Bernard Shaw

IN MAY OF 2007, I brought my 27-foot Winnebago Sightseer home and named her Mehitabel. She looked impressive and enormous next to my ranch home. Now I needed to get comfortable driving her. I was planning a three-month shakedown cruise to start in November, but there was a lot to do and a couple of shorter trips before then.

The name Mehitabel is from the book *Archy and Mehitabel* by Don Marquis, which my mother had loved. Archy, a philosophical cockroach, was the typist; Mehitabel was an alley-cat in her ninth life. Amid whatever chaos was happening at our house, Mother frequently quoted from *The Song of Mehitabel*. The poem is too long to include here, but here are Mother's favorite lines:

wotthehell wotthehell
there s a dance in the old dame yet
toujours gai toujours gai

Was I ever frightened of this adventure I was about to undertake? You bet. I've been scared many times in my life: my first divorce, raising two boys alone, moving to North Carolina. Fear comes up whenever I face something new, but I understand that it's all in my mind. I've tried to use my mind to get rid of the fear, but that doesn't work. It seems the only way to get over it is to expose myself to whatever it is that's causing it. So, yes, I was afraid, but I was determined to push through that fear and was unbelievably excited, thinking about life on the road. I never wanted to let fear define me for long, except for my fear of heights—no sky-diving or bungee-jumping for me.

Driving Mehitabel was terrifying at first. My shoulders were up around my ears, driving her home. It required every bit of my focus to maneuver in traffic, turn corners, ignore the cars in the lanes next to me that seemed way too close. After a couple of hours, though, the tension would dissipate, I could listen to the radio, and realize driving an RV was not so hard—most of the time anyway. I learned to be careful when choosing a gas station for fill-ups; driving up to the pump wasn't bad, but there needed to be enough room available to get out as well, especially when towing the car. I never did get over the habit of ducking my head and holding my breath when going under an overpass.

The first short adventure was the September three-day Loners on Wheels (LoWs) East Coast Rally in Marion, North Carolina. I put Bijou in her carrier, strapped her into the passenger seat, and Mehitabel, Bijou, and I were off to join seasoned and new RVers from many states plus Canada. I learned about safe places to camp overnight for free, like Walmart, and Flying J. And I heard about the wonders of Quartzsite, Arizona, where thousands of RVers from the midwest and northeast gather in the winter to escape icy weather.

An 86-year old gentleman taught line dancing each morning. I learned (sort of) how to do the *Electric Slide, Elvira,* and *Waltz Across Texas.* It was great fun, but it was clear I would never be a skilled line dancer.

There were plenty of activities, more than a dedicated introvert needed, so I occasionally escaped to Mehitabel to read for a while.

After an early breakfast on my last morning, I went out to dump Mehitabel's holding tanks. The sewer hose was stretched to the max due to my sloppy parking job. When I opened the valve to the black-water tank, the other end jumped out of the drain, spewing the water and poop all over. So thankful no one was around to witness my embarrassment, I used Bijou's pooper scoop to clean up the mess. Yuck! I must park closer to the drain in the future. And, oh yeah, on this trip, the backup camera stopped working.

Shortly after the rally, Bijou and I took Mehitabel up to New England to show her off to my family. This time I didn't use the carrier as Bijou hadn't liked that. Putting the key in the ignition was her signal to head for the back of the rig and crawl up under the bed covers. She'd stay there until I stopped and told her it was safe to come out.

I called ahead to a Walmart in Maryland, but they didn't welcome RVers and suggested the Timonium Fairgrounds. I took their advice, but within 15 minutes of getting set up was kicked out by the security guards. I moved to a nearby Park & Ride lot, right next to the highway. I didn't get much sleep that night due to the traffic noise.

The next morning I discovered things are apt to fly around in an RV as though a poltergeist is at work. I hit a curb going around a tight corner, an overhead cupboard flew open, and plastic dishes cascaded across the floor with a great clatter.

We traveled through Pennsylvania: horse farms, fields of corn all dry and brown, clear blue lakes, and lots of trees, some of them starting to show autumn golds and reds. We took secondary roads to detour through Amish country, with its peaceful farms and horse-drawn buggies moving at century-old speeds. That created a problem as there was seldom room to pass, and there were no turnouts where I could stop for a break. Finally, back on the highway, we arrived at Winding Hills State Park in Montgomery, New York, a charming spot in dense woods on Diamond Lake.

The following day I arrived in New Hampshire and a big, old three-family-home, which my son Brian owns. I backed Mehitabel into his parking lot and jumped out to hug Brian and my ten-year-old granddaughter, Brianna. She spent the night with me and darn near turned into a popsicle. I had not yet figured out that there was a furnace plus a thermostat. Nor had I anticipated the rig would get so cold when the temperature dropped.

Leaving Nashua, I drove to Westborough, Massachusetts, to show off Mehitabel proudly to my dad, who was in an assisted-living facility there. He was impressed with the RV, though concerned when I told him of my plan to take a three-month vacation from my business and drive across the country with Bijou. It was always so heart-warming to see my dad; he was in his late 80's, still in good shape, though it was evident he was slowing down.

The next stop was Rutland to see my brother Jonathan and his family. I stayed at a campground, a little on the seedy side, in town. The slide-out had been giving me trouble but extended with no problem. He and his wife, Annemarie, came over that evening to visit. In the morning, getting ready to leave, the slide-out wouldn't retract. Supposedly, you can crank it in by hand, but that didn't work either. I was stuck, trying to find someone to come out and fix it with no success. Jonathan came by after work, and we finally managed to muscle it in.

On the following day, I stopped for gas a bit south of Hartford and noticed the outside rear tire was flat and off the rim. It's a good thing there were double tires in the rear, or my RV adventure might have ended abruptly on the highway.

I cautiously drove over to a nearby tire dealer, spent $300, and sat around for a couple of hours while the tire got replaced. As I paid, I realized I could have called AAA and used my spare. I hoped these mishaps meant my trip to New Mexico would be uneventful.

Late that afternoon, I got to Allentown, Pennsylvania, and found a Walmart. Two huge trucks were parked near me at the far end of the lot, running their growling diesel engines all night. I felt like they were my guardians, keeping me safe.

Once home, Mehitabel had to spend time at the dealer, getting a new backup camera and a new motor at one end of the slide-out.

On November 20, we were on our way west at last—Mehitabel, Bijou, and me—with the dinghy this time, driving through a golden, russet, and olive-green world toward New Mexico. I had met a big bear of a guy, Ken, at the Rally, also heading to the southwest, so we planned to caravan together. I had been feeling a bit anxious at this enormous undertaking, so it gave me a measure of comfort to know someone with more experience would be along. We met up at a rest area in Winston-Salem and went over some ground rules—top speed about 60, stop every hour or two, end the day about four. Much to my dismay, none of the rules got followed after the first leg of the journey.

We stopped for gas in Asheville, had dinner at a Cracker Barrel, and drove until eight, stopping for the night at a rest area in the mountains, right on the Tennessee line. Traffic noise all night, but not too bad, and the sunrise was lovely as it touched on the golds and rusts of the trees.

Ken was under orders from his family to spend Thanksgiving with them in Knoxville. We spent the next two nights parked next to their big barn, 100 head of cattle, and two adorable and shy donkeys, and managed to have three Thanksgiving dinners with various family members. Thanksgiving night was cold. At 6:30 in the morning, my furnace sputtered and stopped. The lights on the levels panel (also known as *idiot lights*) indicated there was no propane left, and the battery was almost dead. I started the engine to recharge the battery and went to tell Ken. After 40 minutes, I was all charged up. Note to self: if I'm boondocking and need heat and lights at night, I'd need to run the generator periodically to charge the batteries—another learning experience.

On our way again, Ken leading, we drove almost 400 miles, the last 100 or so at 70 mph. I was steamed about the speed as it's not safe to go that fast in an RV. I kept trying to call Ken on the CB, but he didn't answer. I should have pulled off the highway and traveled the rest of the way alone.

Finally, we stopped at an outlet mall a little east of Memphis to figure out where the nearest Walmart was. That was where Mehitabel died. Getting ready to take off again, I turned the key. There was nothing but a click. I called AAA, a guy came out and replaced the battery, but it didn't make any difference. We spent the night right there.

The next morning, AAA got busy to find a place that could fix me up on Thanksgiving weekend. The only one they found was Mann's Wrecker Service in Jackson, Tennessee—67 miles in the wrong direction. It was a repair business, so they might be able to solve my problem. If not, since a couple of the service people would be there, they would let Bijou and me stay in the RV over the weekend, for which I was extremely grateful.

Ken took off, heading for warmer weather. I didn't blame him, but your caravan partner is supposed to stick with you. I  waited for the wrecker and followed it back to Jackson in my car. It's so depressing to see your RV towed down the highway. When we got there, he pushed Mehitabel into a corner of their lot and left her, still hooked up to the tow truck. I parked my car and joined Bijou. Their guys worked on Mehitabel, but after two hours couldn't find the problem, so Bijou and I settled in for a cold, rainy, bleak Thanksgiving weekend.

I took a shower and washed my hair. The furnace and water heater were both running. The CO detector in the bedroom went off, so I opened windows and turned on the bathroom fan, then turned off the furnace. Finally, it stopped. But it went off a couple more times, so I removed the battery and hoped I'd live through the night.

Still alive the next morning, I got out of bed and shoved the thermostat way up to warm the place, then crawled back under the covers. Within five minutes, the furnace stopped.

I gave up, and got dressed, then tried starting the generator but got nothing except chirps. Finally, after a cold breakfast, I fed Bijou and went over to Mann's office to get warm and have coffee.

When I explained my predicament to the super, he had Mehitabel maneuvered over next to the building so I could plug in. Now I had electricity and heat for the balance of my stay. Yay! It was lovely to be warm.

On Monday morning, the wrecker towed me west to Chuck Hutton Chevrolet in Memphis and left me there. It turned out the ignition had melted, probably because of the high-speed driving. Thanks, Ken.

At 4:00 P.M. on November 26, I was on my way again, with a brand-new ignition system. Twenty minutes out of Memphis, a rock—or a bullet—hit my windshield and created a starburst right next to the center divider. Yikes! Was the Universe trying to send me a message? It was starting to seem that way. I decided to ignore it.

After crossing the Mississippi River, I parked that night at a Walmart in Forrest City, Arkansas. Worried about the furnace and battery, I didn't sleep well, but everything was fine.

Ken had called to tell me there was going to be snow on I-40, and I should head south, so I spent some time with the map to plan a new route. The next morning, I drove down through Arkansas, a watery state with flat fields of standing water, shallow ponds, and swamps.

Crossing into Texas at Texarkana, I suddenly had a feeling of tremendous exhilaration. It felt like something inside me was expanding, opening up a marvelous sense of freedom. I thought Aunt Nita must have felt like this when taking the train to her first summer in Wyoming. I felt utterly and wonderfully alive in a new way. Such an incredible sensation; I knew I was doing the right thing, heading out into the unknown on my own. If you have ever had this feeling, that is your internal GPS telling you you're on the right track.

So keep going! My heart has always pulled me West. Those seven summers on the ranch in Wyoming when I was young, left a lasting impression.

I was now traveling through the ranching part of Texas, and there were vast ranges of cattle and horses. Occasionally, there was a big, fancy gate with a baronial mansion at the end of a long drive. I continued to Caddo Mills KOA campground east of Dallas.

On November 28, I journeyed around Dallas and kept heading west. It was a beautiful day, and I was thrilled to be doing this despite the problems I'd had.

The landscape got more exciting on the last day of driving. All I could see were mountains and vast empty plains. I was now in the Chihuahuan Desert.

··· 3 ···

My Late-Blooming Hippie Phase

The real voyage of discovery consists not in seeking new landscapes but in having new eyes. — Marcel Proust

I ARRIVED AT LoW-Hi ranch in Deming, New Mexico, on November 29, parked, unhooked the car, hooked Mehitabel up to power and sewer, left Bijou asleep under the covers, and went into town to re-stock with groceries. Then I vacuumed, had a much-needed shower, and stopped in at the ranch's daily happy hour. There I met a guy about my age named Hal. He seemed nice, looked to be in good shape (many of the other men in the group weren't), had a Class C RV, and wasn't towing a car. We struck up the usual conversation: Where are you from? Where are you going? How long have you been RVing? I figured I'd be seeing him again.

One morning, rain and wicked winds woke me up at four. Mehitabel was rocking and rolling. The wind continued the following day, but the rain stopped. Hal came by, and we decided to take my car to Rockhound State Park after lunch. We drove into Spring Canyon as well and saw some Ibex up on the cliffs, goats originally from Iran. I never did learn how they got to New Mexico.

Hal and I went out to dinner a couple of times—actual dates. He had been planning to leave the end of the month but changed his mind.

I bought a five-gallon propane tank plus an adapter and filled it up when the big propane truck came through the park. I got it all hooked up, and lit the stove to verify gas was coming through but didn't use gas during the day as I had an electric heater to use while plugged into power. I set the thermostat at 60 when I went to bed and heard the heat come on a couple of times but woke at 1:30, freezing—it was 50 degrees. I started the furnace up and crawled back into bed, but it stopped again in a few minutes. I tried once more with no better results, so set up the electric heater aimed into the bedroom. In the morning, I went outside to check and found I'd left the valve in the closed position. There's certainly a lot to learn about RV living.

On a bright blue-sky day, Hal and I took my car and drove to Silver City, where we had lunch at a Mexican restaurant, then wandered through quaint little art galleries.

Hal tended to talk nonstop on these drives, reading the signs out loud and punctuating his announcements with laughter as though everything he said was funny. I found it tiring. Also, I felt uncomfortable as he frequently said or did things to indicate we were a couple. I didn't particularly want us to be, though I did enjoy having someone with whom to hike and explore. I'd spent the past 25 years or so alone, so I found parts of this togetherness difficult and annoying.

Every Tuesday, a group of us from the campground went to lunch at The Pink Store in Paloma, Mexico. It's a big Mexican restaurant and gift shop, with stained glass hanging from the ceilings, blown glass ornaments, jewelry, glassware, and pottery. As we didn't have Mexican car insurance, we parked at the border and walked across.

We all sat at a long table and got our first Margarita free. The LoWs had an ongoing relationship with the owners of The Pink Store, and they always treated us well. Two or three Mexican men, with big sombreros and bright, sparkly jackets, played accordion and guitars and sang, so sometimes we danced.

On another day, Hal and I went to Truth or Consequences. An internet site I'd been playing with, FindYourSpot.com, indicated this was the number one spot for me, but I didn't care for it. The landscape was ugly, with hills and close-by mountains, and the town had a sad feeling in some way. Silver City, another recommendation, looked more exciting and had a livelier art scene.

I did a little drawing late one afternoon and was anxious to start painting, though I kept putting it off for one reason or another. There were some lovely sunrises and sunsets, but gusty winds made it impossible to set up painting gear outside. That wind was pretty much a constant in these parts, so I had to rely on taking photos.

The Florida Mountains were nearby, and we climbed one of the lesser peaks one beautiful day. Golden dried grasses and tiny sage bushes covered the side of the mountain. The air was crystal-clear, with puffy clouds, and you could see forever. We sat on a rock at the top, listening to the occasional bird calls, and drinking it all in.

I had started an online, drop-ship business with bird-related products—bird baths, feeders, houses—to bring in some money. One morning I got up early, checked Gmail while eating breakfast, and had my first two orders. It took a while to figure out what to do, but I finally got the orders sent off to the drop-shipper. Unfortunately, when I had added these products to my site, I had forgotten to put them on the list for shipping charges. So I had to pay those fees, which ate up my profit. Oh well.

Coveys of Gambel's quail ran here and there on our walks. Almost every evening, I heard coyotes yelping. Just before sunrise, I could listen to donkeys braying and roosters crowing. Early in the morning, the blinds in my bedroom flushed with rose, then gold, as the sun came up from behind the Floridas.

I was in a delayed hippie phase, falling in love with this landscape of strange plants: boxing glove, Gila cactus, yucca, and snakeweed, those perfectly round mounds that dot the plains. The yucca grows taller as it ages, new growth only at the top; the older leaves, gray and dried, lie against the stalk, like an old woman's hair. All the plants have thorns.

On several mornings there were marvelous feathers of frost on the roof and windshield of my car. On one of our drives, I had to laugh when I saw a bumper sticker: *Fasten your seatbelts. It makes it harder for the aliens to suck you out of your car.* New Mexico is the land of UFOs.

··· 4 ···

Burning Bridges

If we don't change, we don't grow. If we don't grow, we aren't really living. — Gail Sheehy: American author

MID-DECEMBER HAL AND I went up to Silver City for lunch, then drove about two hours out to the Gila Cliff Dwellings National Monument. The road is twisting and narrow, climbing up, then descending, with breathtaking views. At one point, we were at 7,440 feet elevation. We got to the monument and hiked or climbed the path up to the caves, then down again.

I was bothered by some things about Hal, but there were several positive aspects to the situation as well. He knew more about maintaining engines than I did, and it was great to have a friend for hikes and adventures. I was enjoying myself, and we laughed a lot. He had not been part of my plan, but for the time being, I decided to relax and see how it went.

I tended to get anxious if I didn't get time to work on my website, but told myself: *Don't blow it. Learn to deal with the days that work doesn't get done and be okay with it. What you're doing is long overdue and very much needed in your life.* It was challenging to break the habits of 25-odd years of living alone; change is difficult, but I knew it was necessary.

There was a Christmas party at The Pink Store, and that evening another party and gift exchange at the Rec Hall. We had lots of fun, trading and stealing gifts. A bottle of Bacardi and one of wine were the most popular ones. Many of the campers were heavy drinkers.

On Christmas Day, the ranch had a big potluck dinner with ham, turkey, and lots of side dishes. Hal and I sat with another couple; afterward, the four of us went to Hal's rig to drink wine, take photos, and laugh. The day was lots of fun, until the end anyway.

About 10:30, I went back to my rig to find the filtered water spigot running and water all over the floor. Several feet of carpet had gotten sopping wet. The sink wasn't overflowing, so I wondered where the water was coming from, then discovered Bijou's litter box floating in the shower pan, which was full of water. It finally dawned on me to check the holding tank level. It indicated full, of course, so I went out into the blustery wind to dump the tanks. The compartment lid kept banging down on my head.

It took me until midnight to drain the shower and sop up as much water as possible. I finally climbed into bed, where Bijou had been hiding when I came home. She knew something was wrong. Did she turn on the faucet? Maybe I knocked it on when I left earlier. It took me a long time to get to sleep.

I borrowed a wet vac the next morning and sucked up more water, with my fingers crossed there would be no significant damage.

At the end of December, we fled the cold snap in southwest New Mexico and headed for Arizona. The drive was beautiful. I had never realized that there were so many mountains in the southwest before this adventure. We arrived at Double Adobe RV Ranch, a few miles from Bisbee, and decided to stay for a month.

We sat and watched a gorgeous sunset while having a drink, then had dinner and watched a movie, grateful to be in Arizona, and out of the cold in New Mexico.

Bisbee is a neat little historic town in the Mule Mountains, populated with nearly 5,200 recovering hippies and built on the side of a mountain, next to vast open pits and piles of tailings left over from the  copper mining days. The houses and various buildings stagger up the side of Tombstone Canyon like Victorian matchboxes. We had lunch at the Bisbee Grill, then sat in the sunshine on the porch of the Copper Queen, a beautiful old, haunted hotel. There are lots of art galleries and antique shops in town.

On another cold and windy day, we drove to Tombstone and wandered through shops looking for cowboy boots. Hal likes to bargain (I don't) and didn't buy the nice ones he found, but I was all set to buy a pair I found, along with a belt. He wouldn't let me pay for them, so I decided I'd buy a ring instead. He ended up paying for that as well. It made me uncomfortable, so I insisted on treating him to dinner at the Copper Queen that night. We had a delicious dinner and enjoyed talking about the history of the hotel with one of the owners.

Another day, we drove to Douglas and walked over the border to the town of Agua Prieta in Sonora, Mexico, to have lunch and shop.

Hal was determined to buy a pair of boots, so we wandered until we found a boot store. He ended up with a nice pair for half the price he had paid for mine. He couldn't negotiate them down, though he tried.

That night he had a flood in his Tioga. He had left the faucet dripping in case the temperature plunged but had forgotten to leave the gray-water tank open. When we opened the curtains in the morning and looked across at his rig, water was dripping everywhere. He borrowed a wet vac and left it to dry out for several days.

Whitewater Draw is a wildlife refuge not far from Double Adobe. A big lake with trails all around it provides winter habitat for 17,000 sandhill cranes along with snow geese and owls. We went there one afternoon and took some beautiful photos against the backdrop of a dark, stormy sky striped with rainbows.

A few days later, we made a second visit as the sun was setting and strolled out to a stand of trees where all the owls hung out. Several of them flew silently over me, their undersides all white, looking like angels.

On a second trip to Douglas and Agua Prieta, Hal turned out to be quite a shopper. He got three Western shirts, a belt, and a big fancy buckle, negotiating prices on each. I didn't enjoy having to stand around and watch. Next time, I'd let him go alone.

We visited Chiricahua National Monument about 75 miles away. It's a fantastic place, quiet and woodsy, with incredible rock formations like spiraling towers, precariously balanced. Water and wind have eroded the rock vertically, and there are many freestanding columns and pinnacles. A classic *sky island*, once the Apache stronghold of Geronimo, the monument is now a birdwatchers' paradise. You can find nearly 400 species there. There are 300 miles of trails criss-crossing the Chiricahuas, the most extensive mountain range in southern Arizona.

We enjoyed our month at Double Adobe, though cell and internet signals were unreliable, which made it difficult to get work done on my computer. At the end of January, we headed back to LoW-Hi in Deming.

In early February, a dust-storm hit us with gusts to 45 mph. We could see nothing but a brownish haze in every direction. When it finally stopped, the sun illuminated the near end of the Floridas, which were coated entirely with sand. Fine dust had seeped through Mehitabel's window frames, and fine grit covered the inside ledges.

We went to Silver City on our last weekend and ate lunch at Vicki's Café, then drove out route 152 by the Chino mine, and highway 61 along the Mimbres River. We stopped for a bit at City of Rocks State Park—an other-worldly looking place, with lots of big rocks sticking up in the middle of a flat plain.

On February 17, I pointed Mehitabel east toward North Carolina, homeward bound. My shakedown cruise was over. I was ready to close my business and sell my house. There was a lot to do, and I was anxious to get the ball rolling.

Hal followed me in his rig. (I'm not sure how that decision was made—I don't remember inviting him.) We took I-10 to Texas, picked up I-20, and continued through Louisiana, Mississippi, and Alabama. I didn't keep notes of the journey and can barely remember it. My mind was on what lay ahead. I do remember we got lost somewhere around Atlanta. Once we sorted that mess out, we continued on I-20, picking up I-95 in Georgia, and I-40 in North Carolina for the last leg into Raleigh.

Within two weeks, the *For Sale* sign went up in front of my house. I priced it aggressively, and in another two weeks, it was under contract. I got busy selling and giving away the last of my possessions. I also had a lunch meeting with my agents and told them the news. An agent from our original group had started a firm of her own the previous year, so the others had a new broker ready and waiting for them.

Hal was a big help, cleaning up the yard and shed, pitching in wherever he could. It wasn't easy for him to be at my house. Both of us were exhausted much of the time. I had a lot on my mind; I'm not sure what was on Hal's mind. He had brought a big suitcase in from his RV and seemed paranoid about it; he kept asking for reassurance that I would not open it. There were some bad moments, but we struggled through them, and I decided to ignore a couple of incidents that bothered me.

Then, one evening, he asked, "Would you get rid of Bijou?"

His question surprised and troubled me. "Hal, she's been with me longer than you have; she's an important part of my family and my sense of home, and I'm not going to give her away." He appeared to accept that, but I had an uneasy feeling.

I had been in Raleigh for almost 20 years. I was sad to be leaving some special friends behind, but I was looking forward to Minnesota and more travel adventures to come.

On April 28, 2008, I closed on my house. We caravanned our RVs up to Falls Lake just north of Raleigh for three lovely days of rest before starting the trek to Minnesota. It looked like rainy weather ahead.

··· 5 ···

Exploring Minnesota

Go confidently in the direction of your dreams.
Live the life you have imagined. — Henry David Thoreau

WITH THE HOUSE sold, I was footloose; there was no *home* to go to anymore. That knowledge was both exhilarating and a bit disconcerting. *Home* now meant Bijou and Mehitabel.

On May 2, we left Falls Lake, and our two RVs headed west on I-40. We stopped at a Camping World to get air in my tires, and the service guy pointed out severe cracking around the rims, which could result in a blowout. The thought of a blowout in Mehitabel struck fear in my heart, but the cost of replacing them

at Camping World would be about $1,800. Hal thought it would be safe to put it off until we got to Minnesota. I decided to wait, but it made me nervous.

We had a beautiful drive through the mountains and stopped for the night at a Walmart east of Knoxville. The next morning, we had a wild ride up through Tennessee into Kentucky, with gusting wind and pouring rain. With the rain drumming on the roof, the tires splashing through water on the road, and the low growl of Mehitabel's engine, it was a noisy trip. The storm intensified all the colors; redbud trees were starting to bloom, their hot pink blossoms intermingled with the green of the trees.

We stopped for lunch at the Kentucky Artisan Center, a Travelers' Rest Area filled with arts and crafts, then drove for another two hours, My hands were tense, gripping the steering wheel, as the wind tried to push Mehitabel around. Finally, we pulled off the highway at a rest area in Indiana. I was exhausted, and we decided to stay for the night. After all, it was still cold in Minnesota; there was no need to hurry.

The next day we traveled to Bloomington, Illinois, and pulled into the most delightful Walmart lot I'd ever seen. It was well off the highway, and all their spring flowers were out on the lot. It had finally stopped raining; the air was fresh and dry, filled with the scent of all those flowers. We walked to a nearby Mexican restaurant for a dinner of fajitas and collapsed into bed about eight. It was the soundest sleep I'd had in weeks.

On May 5, we stayed at Little Yellow River Campground in New Lisbon, Wisconsin, with showers, electric, the works. I remember lots of mosquitos.

In all the rest areas, I had noticed truck drivers walking little dogs—usually poodles or dachshunds. They talked to their dogs as they wandered around. It must be a lonely life, driving a big truck back and forth across the country. I liked to see them enjoying their canine companions.

On May 6, we crossed the mighty Mississippi River at La Crosse. There was no shortage of water in this part of the U.S. It had been a long, cold, snowy winter and, so far, a thoroughly wet spring.

In Hal's hometown in Minnesota, a friend had given us the okay to park on his land. We pulled our rigs into his emerald green field, with a view of a small lake, then went to Hal's apartment to get his car. Over the next few weeks, Hal emptied his apartment, selling and giving stuff away.

Once, we took a much-needed day off and drove up to Minnehaha Falls in Minneapolis, in a beautiful park with spreading oaks, flower gardens, and lush green lawns. The next stop was the Mall of America. What a fantastic place! There's an amusement park, with a roller-coaster no less, under a glass roof at the center of the mall, plus every store and fast-food eatery you could imagine.

Finally, we had Mehitabel packed up and ready to head north. After the wet spring, she was stuck in the mud, so we got a farmer to pull her out with his truck.

This part of southern Minnesota is farmland. There are vast fields everywhere; the topsoil is 20 inches deep; after plowing, the earth is a rich burnt umber. In some spots, the land rises away on both sides of the road, swelling up like waves to meet the sky. It feels like you are standing at the very top of the planet. Three weeks after planting, the rows of corn were about six inches high. There were grassy areas and fields of oats or alfalfa, a brilliant emerald green, and the woods were thick with big deciduous trees. The only evergreens we saw were near homes, planted as windbreaks.

Driving north, we left the farmland behind. The land became rockier, and red and white pine mixed with the deciduous trees.

We arrived at Jay Cooke State Park in the early afternoon. It's a gorgeous park on the St. Louis River, 20 miles south of Duluth. The river rushes through a narrow gorge of slate, wrackstone, and shale, tipped on edge as the earth folded. The root beer-colored water was high from all the rain. We took a walk across the swinging bridge and along the river, snapping photos of the raging water.

At Black Bear Casino, I lost $17 of my poker winnings (I almost always won our many poker games). Hal lost a couple of hundred dollars but didn't seem to mind.

One day after lunch, we took the car up to Duluth on the shore of Lake Superior. It was windy and cold, but it wasn't raining, and there were glimpses of sun and blue sky. We had a drink and snack at Grandma's Saloon next to the Canal, hoping to see a 1,004-foot long ore carrier. Unfortunately, it was ahead of schedule, so we missed the best part, where the famous aerial lift bridge rises straight up over the canal. We did see the ship as it left, headed out to open water.

Hal took me to Black Woods for a yummy dinner. He described the men's room where men stand at tall urinals filled with ice. Over each urinal is a porthole looking out at the people in the bar. So, the guy gets to ogle pretty women as he's whizzing on the ice. Sadly, there wasn't anything like that in the women's room.

On June 11, we headed for Ely, on the edge of the Boundary Waters Canoe Area Wilderness. There, we made camp at Fall Lake Campground in Superior National Forest.

A couple of mornings later, we took the car and left camp, drove east, then north on Highway 61, stopping in Grand Marais, Minnesota, at a lovely harbor. We walked over the rocks and out onto the seawall at Artists' Point. A wedding party was coming back from a picture-taking session, and the bride looked mighty chilly. Lake Superior was just plain awesome.

It was a glorious day on the shore of the lake. We'd had rain and wind every day or night for the past two weeks, so it was delightful to be in the sunshine. We continued north, all the way to Grand Portage State Park on the Canadian border.

We hiked up the trail to High Falls on the Pigeon River, where water (3,200 gals/second) tumbled 120 feet down the cliff and created a double rainbow. The heavy spray drenched us, but it felt beautiful.

We visited the International Wolf Center in Ely, an experience I had been eagerly anticipating, as I've always believed I was a wolf in a previous existence. Goosebumps popped up on my arms, and my eyes filled with tears seeing the exhibits. The center had acquired two new wolf pups one week earlier. They were born on April 27 and weighed nine pounds each. We watched them play while they were with their human *nannies* in a large playpen inside. When their social hour was nearing an end, the four adult wolves outside started waking up and walking toward the windows. When the door opened, the pups scampered out to their side of the double fence, and adults and youngsters exchanged enthusiastic greetings. It was so sweet to watch them. I went again one week later; their weight had doubled.

We also went to the National Bear Center, which had just opened. The big male, Ted, weighed in at 789 pounds, which is quite overweight. The female, Honey, only showed up for a minute. She doesn't pay much attention to the people, but Ted likes people better than he likes other bears. There was also an eighteen-month-old, Lucky, who exhibited typical toddler behavior, running back and forth, playing with toys and Ted, and splashing in the pond.

On Saturday night, we went to the Grand Ely Lodge for a drink and ended up crashing a wedding reception that featured a DJ and music. No one minded that we enjoyed a few dances; at least they didn't throw us out.

We rented a canoe one afternoon, paddling around a big island and fishing unsuccessfully. Another day we fished for three hours at the foot of the Kawishiwi Falls, standing on a prominent outcropping of rock. I caught five walleye—about 1.5 to 2.25 pounds each. Hal got two walleye and a smallmouth bass that he released. He would have gotten more, but I kept him busy, putting the leeches on my hook and unhooking the fish I caught. We ate yummy fresh pan-fried fish for dinner that night.

... 6 ...

Ignoring Another Warning

When someone shows you who they are,
believe them the first time. — Maya Angelou

WE LEFT ELY and headed back toward Duluth. At
Tetagouchee State Park, we hiked out to Shovel Point, high
up on the cliff with amazing views of vast Lake Superior. I
couldn't get my mind around the fact that it's a lake, not an
ocean. We broke up our driving during the day with more
hikes at Split Rock Lighthouse and Gooseberry Falls.

Parked for two nights at the Walmart in Duluth, we
spent time exploring the town. We wandered through Leif
Erickson Park, where the lilacs were in full bloom, along with
wild roses and pinks. The smell was divine. From the park, we
saw one of the big 1,000-foot ore ships leaving the harbor,
fully loaded and riding low on the water.

On June 23, we arrived in Nerstrand Big Woods State
Park, where we spent a little over a month in a lovely shaded

spot at the edge of the woods. On Sundays, the park emptied, leaving just a few of us campers during the week; on Friday afternoons, it filled up again.

With few exceptions, the weather was terrific, so we walked almost every morning and evening in the woods. One day, we saw three adult wild turkeys and 17 little ones crossing the road. The little ones were so funny as they scurried across; one lagged, so an adult, looking a bit impatient, had to go back to fetch him.

The corn was *knee-high by the 4th of July*, so the farmers were happy. The green fields of corn, oats, and soybeans stretched as far as the eye could see. The wind blew, generating waves that traveled through the crops. Wild oats and timothy grass lined the roads, and the ferns were waist high in the woods. There was a fresh, green smell in the air.

We had been practicing with Bijou on the retractable leash, and she was getting better. One day I took her for a walk, the handle slipped out of my hand and fell, which startled her. She took off, and the handle followed, bouncing through the brush. Terrified, she dashed under Mehitabel, the leash wrapped around a tire, and she slipped the collar/chest rig and was off, finally hiding behind a rock.

We tried to coax her back, but when scared, she becomes demonic. When I reached for her, she let out a blood-curdling howl, hissed, and swiped at me with claws extended. Finally, we left her alone, and she spent the night on the platform created by the slide-out.

The next morning, we left the door open and ignored her. She finally crept back in and sneaked into the bedroom. She wouldn't allow us to go near her but, a couple of times, she came and rubbed against my leg, still not letting me touch her. This behavior occurred every time she got scared. She liked to get out and occasionally escaped, but something about being out resulted in her being terrified. It generally took a full twenty-four hours for her to settle down.

We visited Wabasha, the oldest town in Minnesota, and the first one settled west of the Mississippi. It is home to the National Eagle Center, which houses three big, magnificent bald eagles and one golden eagle. All had been injured and were unable to fly, so they could not return to the wild.

Hal's car was all-wheel-drive, so he needed a trailer and traded his boat for one. I was grateful for my standard shift Corolla—loading and unloading his vehicle on the trailer was a lot of work.

In early August, we left Minnesota at last. The corn was now well over our heads, and we'd eaten it several times—fresh from the farm, so tender and sweet. We had taken only Mehitabel for the Ely trip, but we headed off to South Dakota with both RVs, which was starting to make less and less sense. Hal put a *For Sale* sign in the window of his rig. We spent three nights at an RV park in Sioux Falls so I could get my driver's license and register to vote. I'd had South Dakota plates on both my vehicles since the end of May.

We expected Sioux Falls to be some kind of fancy cowtown, so we were delighted to discover it is a pretty cosmopolitan city. There were good restaurants, an active arts community, and an excellent medical center. The town was named for sev-

eral levels of falls on the Big Sioux River, which runs through a park, surrounded by cliffs and out-croppings of pink quartzite.

We left Sioux Falls and spent one night at Oahe State Park, just below the dam on the Missouri River. It's a lovely location, but the mosquitoes were fierce. They fogged the whole area in the late afternoon. I held my breath and hoped the chemicals wouldn't kill us.

On August 9, we drove across rolling hills on Hwy 14, passing wheat fields, cows and horses, stacks of beehives, and acres of sunflowers. There were great rolls of hay, sometimes scattered across the land as though tossed by a giant, other times grouped or stacked in long rows.

We saw scads of motorcycles; this was the week of the big rally in Sturgis, South Dakota. We stopped in the town of Wall to visit Wall Drugs, a small-town drugstore which became famous for the free ice water they offered to weary travelers. More than two million visitors stop here for a rest on the way to attractions like Mt. Rushmore. We had lunch among all the bikers. Ice water is still free.

Later that afternoon, we arrived at Badlands National Park, where we stayed for four nights. National parks are great for seniors; we get free entrance with a Golden Age pass and half-price camping fees, so our cost was just $5/ night. There were no hookups, but there was water available to fill the tank, restrooms (no showers), and a dump station. The scenery was incredible.

The Badlands are in one of the rapidly shrinking areas of dark skies. One evening a ranger gave a presentation at the amphitheater near our campsite, showing photos he had taken of the stars through a telescope. At ten, he turned off all the lights and gave us an astronomy lesson. Even with a glowing half-moon, we could see the Milky Way and several of the major constellations.

Lights along the concrete path leading to and from the amphitheater attracted toads and bugs. As we left, we discovered a rattlesnake had crawled up on the concrete, hoping for a meal. The ranger poked at it with a stick, encouraging the snake to go elsewhere, which it did, rattling angrily as it slithered away.

We left the Badlands and drove to Hart Ranch, a beautiful member-owned RV resort at the foot of the Black Hills National Forest, just south of Rapid City. We had a promotional price for a three-night stay, during which time we learned about all the benefits of membership. The resort included a lodge, an Olympic pool, tennis courts, WiFi, water aerobics, and a snack bar. The air was dryer, and the nights were chilly, plus the park was lovely, well cared for, and quiet. We both felt we could happily stay for a month or so in spring and fall. Hal wanted to buy in; I thought it was too soon to make that decision as we had barely started our travels.

On August 19, everything changed. Hal had gone off to have a few beers. He came back and made an announcement.

"I got a great deal on membership in the non-pet area. I took the *For Sale* sign out of my rig; I'm going to move it there tomorrow and put my trailer in storage. I don't want to live with a cat, and we need some time and space on our own. We can go to Yellowstone in my car and stay in a motel, then come back here and stay until October."

"Wait a minute, Hal. I bought an RV because I didn't want to travel in a car and stay in motels. And I'm not willing to give up my cat. We already talked about that."

"You're choosing the cat over me then."

"Yes, if you want to put it that way. Hal, I had a cat when you met me. We're a package."

I had a bad feeling in the pit of my stomach. He was making decisions without even talking with me. I didn't like that, but I didn't want to bolt if there was a chance for the relationship to work. There were difficulties, but some parts seemed to work well. We did a lot of talking, but it got us nowhere. He kept repeating that I was choosing the cat over him. He'd been having a lot of head and neck pain. I thought that might be part of what was going on. Finally, I asked him to stay away for a couple of days and let me think.

My thoughts went round and round that night. Should I stay or strike out on my own? I knew I wouldn't get rid of Bijou. She gave me a sense of home and had been part of my dream of freedom. I got over being so upset and hurt. Maybe keeping both RVs was a good idea. There was no reason we couldn't go our separate ways at times. After his actions, I wasn't so keen on selling Mehitabel anyway. Frankly, I liked the idea of having more time to myself.

During those long-ago summers on the ranch, Aunt Nita and Hickey taught us to be responsible for ourselves and encouraged our independence. I knew I'd be fine on my own if I made that choice.

We put the discussion aside for the time being. I bought a membership.

I swam laps early in the morning a few times and had the pool all to myself, which was delightful. Ellsworth Air Force Base was about ten miles away; since Hal was retired Air Force, he had access to everything there. The only negative news we'd heard about this area was that it was prone to summer hailstorms.

The resort was near Custer State Park, which we visited several times and loved. We also went to Mount Rushmore National Park (where we saw our first mountain goats) and Crazy Horse Monument. Both places, with their gigantic sculptures, are incredible.

During our three weeks at the park, I got a fishing license. It was inexpensive for me as I was a legal resident of South Dakota now, but it would have cost a lot more for Hal, so he cheered from the bank while I stood in the middle of the creek. My best catch was a 14-inch rainbow trout. Delicious!

One day we took a trip to Hill City. The population was just about 1,300, and most of the residents must have been artists; there were eight art galleries. Another day we took the scenic byway up to Spearfish, stopping in Deadwood on the way back to leave some of Hal's money in the casino.

He moved back in. I was not sure what we were doing, but on September 10, I planned to head west. He hadn't decided whether to come with me in Mehitabel or follow me in his rig.

••• 7 •••

Wyoming & Utah

The geographical pilgrimage is the symbolic acting out of an inner journey. One can have one without the other. It is best to have both. — Trappist Monk Thomas Merton

ON SEPTEMBER 10, we left for Devils Tower, Wyoming. Hal's neck was bothering him again, plus he was getting headaches, which was discouraging. He had decided to follow me in his Tioga, instead of leaving it behind. The electrical cord for my generator had been getting hot, and part of the plug looked like it was melting, so we stopped at Mid-States RV to get it replaced. That killed part of the afternoon, so we spent the night in Spearfish.

On September 11, we arrived at Devils Tower, where we stayed four nights. I had been in Wyoming on September 11, 2001, when the planes crashed into the World Towers. Now here I was again on the anniversary of that horrific event.

I slept little that night, thinking about our situation. It appeared nothing had changed. Though we had two RVs, we were having all our meals in mine, and I was doing all the cooking except grilling. Since he was there every night, I wasn't getting to read or work on my website.

On our walk the next morning, I told him I'd like to have some time to myself two or three nights a week and not be together for every meal.

"We can still use my rig and park yours when we go to a higher-priced campground. That helps us keep costs down, and I enjoy our time together. We can also take the shorter trips in mine as we've been doing. But, when we're both parked at Hart Ranch or National Parks, let's use both houses."

Hal acted shocked by my words, which surprised me since he had been the one to suggest we each needed time and space alone.

It was a pleasant morning, except for that. We hiked around the tower while watching some climbers halfway up. That sure looked scary to me. This part of Wyoming is gorgeous: red rock, fields of golden winter wheat, and that incredible tower rising 865 feet. The pretty Belle Fourché River winds around below it, and there are lots of deer.

That afternoon, we drove into Hulett (population 400) for supplies. Later, Hal took most of his things out of Mehitabel. It was nice to have some of my space back.

Hal didn't sleep well that night. He was angry and bitter about difficulties with his disability compensation (and probably my request for time alone). He had several beers, which got him more depressed and withdrawn.

Our last day, we took a long walk through the prairie dog towns; they are such funny little critters. I had enjoyed my time alone the past couple of days, reading in bed at night, writing in my journal, drawing, and enjoying the silence. It was good for me and made me feel freer. I felt marvelous; I always enjoyed being in Wyoming. I could have sat down out there in the sunshine with the prairie dogs and cried with happiness.

We spent the night of September 15 in Buffalo, Wyoming, and the following day took the Powder River Pass through the Bighorn Mountain Range, elevation 9,666 feet. It was a beautiful drive with just two hairpin turns.

In Cody, we stopped at a Walmart to replace my house batteries, which hadn't been holding a charge very well. We got groceries and left to drive the final 18 miles to Wapiti through a narrow gorge along the Shoshone River. We passed Cody Dam and a vast lake and arrived at last at the Yellowstone Valley Inn RV Park in the Absaroka Mountain Range.

The next morning, we drove through another canyon, alongside the North Fork of the Shoshone River, a drive so lovely I had tears in my eyes half the time. The road into Yellowstone is steep; many miles of going up, up, up at twenty-five miles an hour, with the engine straining like it was gasping for oxygen.

We stayed four nights at Grant Village on Yellowstone Lake, saw Old Faithful go up, and did lots of walking to see the various geysers and pools. I had last seen Morning Glory Pool fifty-three years ago; the name on the sign was now *Fading Glory Pool* as all the trash thrown into it over the years had cooled it down, dulling the colors. What a shame. It makes me sad to see how little care some people have for our natural world.

We saw buffalo, a few herds of elk, and three coyotes walking right along the road with not a care in the world. There were no bears at all. Trash is in bear-proof bins, so bears are not in evidence the way they were when I was a kid, and I missed them. There were signs posted everywhere, warning against leaving anything out, such as food or cosmetics, when you leave camp and at night.

The altitude was challenging in Yellowstone. Our stay at Colter Bay Village, on Jackson Lake, in Grand Teton National Park, was 1,000 feet lower, so more manageable. We stayed for four nights, exploring the surrounding area every day. We spent time wandering the site of the former Half Moon Ranch and my childhood summers. Nothing remains of the ranch now, which breaks my heart. All the buildings and equipment got auctioned off when the park bought it.

The aspens were turning gold; the undergrowth in the woods was full of brilliant yellows, reds, and oranges; the rivers were crystal clear and sparkling blue-green; the air was clean and smelled so fresh. Bijou seemed to be healthier in this dry climate.

Leaving the Jackson Hole area on the 25th, we drove through Hoback Canyon, through southern Wyoming to Evanston, where we intended to spend one night. But, as we checked into Phillips RV, we discovered one tire on Hal's trailer had shredded entirely off the rim. There was a Goodyear dealer next door; they replaced that tire, but it turned out the others were checked and weathered as well, and the valve stems were cracking. So, we ended up staying several days until UPS delivered new tires from the tire company.

The tires arrived on the 29th. Hal was not feeling well. He didn't eat breakfast or lunch but managed cheese and crackers and two or three beers in the late afternoon. I suspected it was emotional rather than physical, and I was running out of words and ideas to get his mind off his problems. He spent that night in the Tioga, which was a relief. I worked on my website that afternoon and evening.

On September 30, we made the lovely drive down into Utah, through mountains with beautiful yellow and orange aspens and rosy, burgundy, and olive shrubbery. It looked as though someone had thrown a multi-colored carpet into the folds of the hills. We spent that night in Provo and made the long drive to Bryce Canyon the following morning. Bryce is a spectacular place with spires of red, gold, white, and orange rock in strange shapes. We hiked the Queen's Walk, which has the least elevation change; only 320 feet down, then up again. Luckily, the sun was playing hide and seek during  our walk, so it wasn't too hot, but it was a challenge coming back up. After lunch, I conked out for a two-hour nap, which was rare for me.

We stayed three nights at Bryce, leaving the morning of October 4, as a bad storm was predicted. We drove down to

Flagstaff through steep red cliffs, pink dunes, and the lavender and gray Vermillion Cliffs. It rained throughout the day, which dulled all the colors, but they were beautiful, nonetheless.

That night we stayed at the Glen Canyon National Recreation Area in Lake Powell, Arizona. The lake was low, surrounded by a weird landscape with cliffs, a Devils Tower look-a-like, and a big power plant in the distance.

Utah gets my vote as the state with the most fantastic landscape, though coming down into Arizona from Lake Powell runs a close second.

There were some confusing moments where we had to set our clocks back and later had to set them forward again. We learned that Arizona does not observe daylight savings time, except for the Four Corners area, where Colorado, Utah, Arizona, and New Mexico all come together.

The next morning, we traveled the last 62 miles to Deming. It was nice to be back at LoWs, seeing old friends. Tuesday, we'd be off to the Pink Store for lunch and our free margarita.

I did some cleaning up and organizing in Mehitabel to make more space for painting. I had so many beautiful photographs and couldn't wait to get started.

Hal and I got into politics one night; we should never do that. He thought Obama was a Muslim and wouldn't listen to evidence to the contrary. He had a closed mind on certain subjects, and he'd had several beers.

At the end of another day, Hal asked me if I wanted to get married. That took me by surprise. Things had been good for a while, and we were comfortable together most of the time. But we sure had our differences, and I knew I tended to ignore my occasional uneasy feelings when all was going well. I said I'd have to think about it.

Part 2

DEAL WITH PROBLEMS & REASSESS

··· 8 ···

Relationships. Are They Worth It?

Do not try to change people; they are only messengers telling you who you are. Revalue yourself and they will confirm the change. — Neville Goddard, Prophet, Teacher and Author

DUE TO RECENT heavy rains, Deming was wonderfully green. Unfortunately, the rain had brought a plague of flies; they were awful, swarms of them just waiting for us to open a door. We became skilled with the swatter.

I got involved with fierce competition in a game called Ladders one afternoon and learned that I was a natural. My team made it to the finals, though we were beaten (barely) at the end. My smooth moves did something to my back. Unable to fix the problem on my own, I went to a chiropractor in town. For $20, he cured my back but really screwed up my neck.

I felt as though we were missing some aspects of RV life by not hanging out more with the other people. It was lots of fun when we did. There were several who were heavy drinkers. Alcoholism may be a problem with retirees in general. It seems they don't have enough to do with their time.

One camper had been drinking for several days, not eating, and ended up in the hospital for a couple of days. When he got out, a good friend was taking care of him, and his kids came. All liquor got removed from his rig. A few days later, he was back in the hospital with a massive infection. On the morning of November 11, he died.

That afternoon, we all met outside his rig, sat around the fire, and talked. It was heartwarming and downright funny at times. Some folks had known him for about ten years, so there were stories of RV caravans to Yuma, to Mexico, to New England. The LoWs group was like a family; they all cared for each other and helped when needed. One of the biggest fears for single people is being alone if we get hurt or ill. Who would take care of us? How would we manage? None of us wants to depend on our kids, most of whom are working hard and dealing with problems of their own. I had not appreciated how supportive the group could be.

I moved Mehitabel over to a boondock site as rates are cheaper without electric and sewer hookups. Temps dropped into the 20s at night. No generators were allowed between ten at night and seven in the morning. I used a lot of gas to run the furnace early in the morning, but I was facing east, so around nine, the sun came through the windshield and finished heating Mehitabel.

Hal brought his whole workmen's comp file over as he needed my help with a letter. I was leafing through it to find the parts of the doctor's report that concerned him, and he pulled the file from me, saying there was information on his health he didn't want me to see because I'd worry. Quite frankly, it was his hiding it that bothered me.

Four of us drove our rigs to Las Cruces for a change of pace and parked for three nights at Walmart. There were NO FLIES in Las Cruces! We visited White Sands National Monument for an afternoon of hiking dunes. What a marvelous place; it was like another world.

Thanksgiving was a big potluck dinner in the recreation hall. To my mind, the best part of Thanksgiving is the leftovers, and we had none. Any self-respecting turkey was too big for the RV oven, so the next day, I bought a chicken, and we took Mehitabel up to City of Rocks State Park to roast the chicken and spend a night. We saw some black-tailed jackrabbits during our walks through the rocks. There was a waxing crescent moon with Venus and Jupiter just two degrees apart that night. The skies are so dark in that part of New Mexico, and they were brilliant with stars.

This park is one of the strangest places I've ever seen and does look like a city of rocks plopped down on a flat plain. They are a type of stone called tuff, made from heat-welded volcanic ash, the fallout from the eruption of Kneeling Nun, 19 miles, and almost 35 million years away.

I had a sale on my website and made about $5. I stupidly invested more money in the hopes that a particular scheme would get my traffic up so I'd start making money. More and more, I felt it was essential to be self-supporting.

There were too many questions about my relationship with Hal. I had real misgivings about it at times. Everything would seem to be going well, and then suddenly it wasn't. Hal thought I was on his case, that I was always criticizing him. He would hold onto that feeling, while I'd said what I wanted to say and forgotten about it already. In time, after a few beers, the things I'd said or done over several weeks would come up. Of course, at that point, he couldn't tell me specifics. I asked him to please tell me when he thought I was criticizing him.

That would alert me to the behavior I needed to watch. Life was certainly a lot simpler when I was not in a relationship, though there were some enjoyable things about being in one. However, there were definite gaps between what I would like it to be and the experience. I needed to communicate my needs better. So did Hal. I knew I tended to be impatient and didn't always stop to consider the best way to say something. Could I change? Could he? When he talked about his past, I noticed he tended to feel a victim. And, there was frequently a disconnect between what he said he would do and his actions. So I couldn't trust his words. That was a problem.

In early December, we started the trek to Yuma, caravanning with our Las Cruces buddies, Sandra and Tom. We stopped at a rest area just over the Arizona line and discovered that Sandra had a broken serpentine belt in her RV. She found a tow truck willing to come out and tow her to Willcox, about 50 miles west of our location. The rest of us followed in our three rigs and parked that night at Dick's Tire & Auto Repair.

We all had a drink in Mehitabel, then walked to the Best Western for another couple of drinks and dinner. Later, Sandra and I tried watching *Desperate Housewives* on my TV, but the reception was terrible. Hal came back from Tom's rig about 8:15 and went to bed shortly after. Sandra left at nine. I wasn't sleepy and told Hal I was going to read in bed as it was too cold to do that upfront. He got upset and left.

The next morning, they got Sandra's rig fixed up, and we were on our way. For the next four nights, we parked at the Desert Diamond Casino in Tucson. Tom and Hal managed to lose some money without trying too hard, and we all did some exploring in the area. We spent most of one day at the Arizona-Sonora Desert Museum, which is a fantastic place; there are exhibits in the buildings, trails through the desert, enclosures with animals native to the area, and enormous saguaro and organ pipe cactus. I loved the large screened building with 16 hummingbirds zooming around like tiny missiles.

We visited several art galleries in north Tucson, and one day drove south to Tubac, a nifty arts community. Parking at the casino was free and fun, except for the fact that we were next to an Air Force Base. F16s kept screaming overhead, which Bijou didn't like at all.

On December 11, we drove about 50 miles and camped at Picacho Peak State Park. We all had much-needed showers that afternoon. Sponge baths are okay, but boy, there's nothing like a hot shower. All our rigs had showers in them, but we tended to use them for storage. Mine was where Bijou's litterbox lived. As the sun went down, we sat with our drinks and watched a long line of commuters coming down I-10 from Phoenix, their headlights like a string of liquid silver beads.

Arizona is a mountainous landscape. In every direction, as you drive across the desert, you see mountain ranges, sometimes several layers of them, fading into the distance. There are long, colorful freight trains crawling back and forth across the desert, usually alongside the highways.

On the 13th, the others headed straight on to Yuma, so our caravan split up. The wind was gusting hard, so Hal and I decided to go halfway, and we camped two nights in Gila Bend at Augie's Quail Trail RV Camp. There's not much happening in Gila Bend.

When we got to Yuma, we headed north on 95 to Martinez Lake, a Marine Corps recreation area next to the Yuma Proving Grounds. We spent two nights there and were awakened the second morning at four by a muffled boom, followed several seconds later by a quieter boom. The Army was doing their tank training; for the next hour, there was a boom every five minutes. It sounded like the Marine's camp was under attack.

It rained intermittently on the 16th and non-stop on the 17th. We hooked up my car in the mud and took off for Quartzsite, where we camped on Bureau of Land Management (BLM) land out in the desert, along with hundreds of migratory RVers known as *snowbirds*. Water and a dump site were available in the area where we camped, and it cost just $40 for a two-week stay. Some RVers come in November and stay until April. It was $180 for a six-month stay.

I had a solar panel installed, with an inverter. I could now run a computer, hairdryer, and TV from the solar panel—pretty much anything other than AC, microwave, or vacuum. So, life was more comfortable. Hal didn't like boondocking as much as I did, so we took turns, dry camping for a while to keep costs down, then going into a campground and paying for amenities like electricity, showers, and laundry facilities. Further down the road into the desert, we heard there was a nudist campground. It seemed a bit chilly for that.

Quartzsite has a population of about 3,000 in the summer, but the number starts swelling in October. There are hundreds of vendors of every kind that set up in the winter months, so it's like a huge flea market. The grocery stores offered only the basics, but 25 miles away, in Blythe, California, was a big supermarket. Mountains surrounded us, and the sunsets and sunrises were glorious.

... 9 ...

Winter In Quartzsite And Yuma

Life is a series of natural and spontaneous changes.
Don't resist them; that only creates sorrow. Let reality be real-
ity. Let things flow naturally forward in whatever way they
like. — Lao Tzu

AFTER A FEW days of gray skies, and alternating intermittent and steady rain, the sun came out, dried up our desert
surroundings, and improved our spirits.

On Christmas Eve, we had Tom and a friend of his over
for dinner. Hal brought out my gift and wanted me to open it
in front of them. I suggested we wait, but he was insistent. So,
we exchanged gifts. Not the way I would have liked to cel-
ebrate our first anniversary. Beware expectations! We should
have discussed this ahead of time. I cannot remember what
we gave each other.

On Christmas Day, we went to the Tyson Wells potluck mid-day and had a great meal with Tom and his friend. After dinner, we watched the two of them fall into lust then we left to have a walk and a nap. Hal slept all afternoon, didn't get up until 6, then went back to bed at 8:30, saying his neck was hurting. It hadn't been a good few days for the relationship.

Christmas week was rocky. We finally sat down together and did some serious talking. Hal had been spending a lot of time drinking with Tom, with predictable results. I finally wrote down my thoughts in a note and gave it to him. In it, I told him I loved him but would choose to go my way if he continued. I had a couple of men in my past with drinking problems, and I didn't want to deal with it. It was not good for him anyway as he had a problem with depression, and drinking made it worse. He knew that. He said he would cut back. I was drinking more than was healthy, so I planned to drink less, as well.

New Year's Resolutions? Let's see:
Yoga: 2/3 times/week; 2-mile walk 4-5 times/week
Booze: cut back—4 evenings/week sounded good
Painting: get to it, girl!
Website: put some real effort into it; either start making $$ or quit
Write: work with the writing books I have and see what I can come up with
Weight: lose 5 pounds. That seems to be on my list every year.

Hal got a spot for his RV at Desert Breeze Travel Camp on the base at the United States Army Yuma Proving Ground (YPG) on January 1. He took his rig there, then came back in his car to stay an extra week with me at one of the 14-day free areas on BLM land in Quartzsite. I was getting more work done on Mehitabel. The windshield crack I got back in '07 had started creeping, so I needed to get it fixed. I also needed a new patio awning and a repair to the sway bar.

I liked living in the desert. It was so peaceful there. Plus, you couldn't beat the price. I was confident Bijou and I could make it on our own, should we ever choose, or need, to do that.

The repair work got finished on the 9th, and I brought Mehitabel down to YPG. Hal put his Tioga in the storage area, and I got hooked up in our spot with water, sewer, and electric. The amenities were great; there was even a small movie theater. We drove down to Yuma to get groceries at the Marine base and had a yummy lunch at Asian Fusion. On the way back, we stopped at a farm stand to get fruit and veggies. All were local, fresh, and delicious looking. There were fields of lettuce and cabbage, orange groves, and date palm orchards along Highway 95. It was nice to see the bright colors after the dulled palette of the desert.

I flew up to San Francisco on January 16 to see Jeff, Laurie, and Jack. We went to the beach twice; the weather was gorgeous. We all watched Jack's first basketball game; Jeff was one of the coaches and seemed perfect for that job.

Laurie's parents came to dinner one night. They are such good grandparents—always thinking of the kids and grand-kids and doing things for them. My first husband is like them. For whatever reason, my internal wiring doesn't work that way. I love to see them and enjoy it when I do, but a little goes a long way. It would be nice if we all lived nearer each other so we could visit more frequently.

We took both rigs to BLM land at the end of January for a couple of weeks. I loved being back in the desert with no close neighbors, plus I could come and go, and shop by myself, things I was unable to do while on the base.

We explored the area, drove up to Lake Havasu City one day, visited Parker Dam, and stopped at Buckskin Mountain State Park on the Colorado River for lunch. The drive through the Buckskin Mountains is beautiful. They are chocolate-colored, and there's an emerald green golf course tucked into a couple of the canyons near the park. Some of the little canyons have palm trees growing in them.

In Lake Havasu City, we went to see London Bridge. Robert McCulloch purchased it from the City of London after it was dismantled. He had the original exterior granite blocks numbered and shipped to America, then reassembled them, piece by piece, over the Colorado River in Lake Havasu City. The city itself is a planned community he developed in 1964.

On the drive back, we stopped at the Bill Williams River National Wildlife Refuge, a gorgeous area with a blue-green river winding through a sea of golden reeds and grass, the chocolate cliffs of the Buckskin Mountains rising above.

Hal took his rig back to Desert Breeze a couple of days before I did. I drove out to Joshua Tree National Park in California after he left. It was chilly and cloudy, spitting rain, and that weather system followed me back to Quartzsite. There were gusty winds with rain off and on all the next day. That can be dismal in the desert, but you can't complain, as it happens so seldom. During the few breaks in the rain, I climbed on the roof, lay the solar panel down, then hooked my car to the towbar, so I'd be ready to leave the next morning. The clouds broke up at the end of the day, and there was a brilliant double rainbow. It was so lovely, with the sun gleaming on the wet creosote bushes. There is a delicious earthy smell in the desert after the rain.

Desert Breeze is the winter training site for the Golden Knights, the Army's parachute team, as well as for the Army Rangers. Almost every day, we saw men and women falling out of planes and opening big gold and white, or red, white, and blue parachutes. Sometimes, they trailed red smoke and did pretty spirals as they came down. They looked to be having a wonderful time up there, and I imagined a few of them would love to stay up and drift off somewhere else. The jumpers all land in Cox Field, a big green field in the center of the base. Folks drive in from all around to watch the show.

One day I watched a big jump. Two planes circled together so high, and about 50 jumped at once, looking like a swarm of bees up there. They did a free-fall for quite a distance, forming a compact star-like design, then one layer at a time let go and moved out, finally leaving five or so jumpers in a small star. When that group let go of their formation, chutes started opening.

How do they manage to all come together after the jump? They must swim through the air. It was amazing to watch, and there were many stiff necks at the end of the day.

I needed new prescription sunglasses and an extra pair of regular glasses, so we took a trip to Los Algodones, across the border in Mexico. The optometrists there promise a two-hour turnaround, so we figured we'd do a little exploring and shopping during the wait. Hah! It takes a minute or two to walk across the border from the US to Mexico, but it's not so easy to get back. We parked on the United States side and walked into Los Algodones, a little border town in the Baja, California area, offering a range of medical services. We arrived about eleven, and couldn't believe it when we saw the line to go back through customs was already halfway down the street. We thought there must have been something special going on that day, but no, it's like that every day during the winter months. Hundreds of people go across for eye doctors, dentists, prescriptions, and liquor. By early afternoon, you can count on standing in line for two or three hours to get back.

I had my appointment, chose my frames, and we went down the street and around the corner to start standing in line. It was 87 degrees and sunny. One lady keeled over into the road and got carted off in an ambulance. There was an awning over about 100 feet of the line, but no cover beyond that. As we neared the final leg, my promised two-hour wait was up, and I left to get my glasses, leaving Hal to hold our place in line. By the time I got back, he was at the door to customs, letting folks go ahead of him. I'm sure I saved a nice amount of money, but next time I'll pay extra and get it done in the states.

We visited the Imperial National Wildlife Refuge and took a drive on a rough dirt road to the Kofa National Wildlife Refuge to see what was blooming. We saw no wildlife, other than a lizard, at either place, though we did see lovely flowers in both areas and along the highway. We saw (and often heard) a coyote outside the fence near Mehitabel.

Spring was starting to arrive in the desert. Since the landscape tends to be various shades of brown and olive green in this part of Arizona, it was encouraging to see brighter colors appearing.

I took a walk one evening; Cox Field looked so peaceful, with long shadows from the palm trees lying across the grass. I was feeling restless and couldn't wait to get out of Desert Breeze. I felt like I was starving for something—art, artists, color, whatever. And I was beginning to detest that chain link fence.

··· 10 ···

Boondocking

Security is mostly a superstition. Avoiding danger is no safer in the long run than outright exposure. Life is either a daring adventure, or nothing. — Helen Keller

IN EARLY MARCH 2009, we left Desert Breeze and drove the 211 miles to Picacho Peak State Park. Lupines and California poppies were blooming in scattered groups, but we didn't see the spectacular display of wildflowers we had anticipated. There hadn't been enough rain over the winter.

We took walks in the evenings to watch the sun go down, and again early in the mornings to see the sun's rays light up the spines on the cholla. A curved bill thrasher sang his song, and jackrabbits raced through the cactus. I liked learning the names of the things we saw: new plants, flowers, birds, and lizards. Google made it easy.

It seemed so quiet in the park, though there was the constant hum of cars on I-10, and at least a dozen trains would go by in 24 hours, each one blowing its mournful whistle.

From Picacho, we traveled to Tucson, and camped out, first at the Desert Diamond Casino, then at Casino del Sol for a bit. We had occasional overnights at RV parks to dump our holding tanks and take a shower.

The second night at Desert Diamond, we moved our rigs into another section of the parking lot to get away from the highway noise. I woke up at two to the sound of growling diesel engines and lights. Three big 18-wheelers had parked in the row in front of me; all their lights were aimed straight at Mehitabel. It turned out we had parked in the truckers' area. We moved back to our old spot in the morning.

We had seen a Winnebago Adventurer we liked while in Quartzsite, so spent a couple of hours at La Mesa RV with Hal negotiating. There was no meeting in the middle. He wanted too much for his RV and would probably need to sell it himself.

We spent my birthday enjoying the art in Tubac, while we stayed at an RV park in Amado. Hal decided to leave his rig there for a few weeks, so we re-organized our belongings and headed back to the casino in Mehitabel. We both won some money—surprise!

Toward the end of March, we drove to Windy Hill Campground at Roosevelt Lake in Tonto National Forest to join the Wandering Individuals Network (WINs) for a ten-day campout. Roosevelt Dam was built on the Salt River between 1903-1911.

The campground sat on a hill above the lake, at the foot of the Superstition Mountains. It was green all around, with palo verde, some saguaros, lots of brittlebush and cactus blooming, and carpets of bright pink owl's clover. Drinking water was available in the campground to fill up water tanks, and there were restrooms with showers, but no electric hook-ups. At night the stars were brilliant.

It was a great time with the WINs. I found them to be an active group with not as much drinking at the four o'clock happy hour or around the campfire later, which was a nice change from Deming. Many of the WINs carried kayaks or canoes on their rigs.

We joined several other cars one day and drove the Apache Trail (Hwy 88), a dirt road, narrow and steep, not meant for RVs. We wound along the Salt River, surprising a herd of bighorn sheep beside the road. At Tortilla Flat, we had lunch and danced to *Peggy Sue, Proud Mary, and Ghost Riders,* played by the energetic Tortilla Flat Band.

Another day, we followed a line of cars on a drive to Four Peaks. I had thought Apache Trail was a challenge; this was worse. Just one lane of gravel or sand, steep, with nothing but a dizzying drop on both sides. I chickened out about halfway to the top, so we turned around and went back.

Mice had gotten into the under-seat compartment where I kept Bijou's food. We set a trap, baited it with peanut butter, and caught four of the little critters over the next few days. That seemed to be the end. I had fond memories of catching field mice in the oat barrel at the Half Moon Ranch and had even kept one as a pet. So, I hated to kill them, but mice and pack rats can do tremendous damage to a car or RV. A couple of the WINs had stories of significant repairs.

There are cliff dwellings at Tonto Monument. We all went hiking up to the Lower Cliff Dwelling one morning but weren't allowed to enter it as there were swarms of African bees.

On April 6, we left Roosevelt Lake and drove through Devil's Canyon to Apache Junction, where we stayed for a night. Onward the next day to a park in north Phoenix, and the following day to Sedona, where I had a coupon for three free nights at a time-share resort. We spent a couple of hours listening to the dog and pony show for the timeshare, but the rest of the time, we explored the beautiful town, took pictures of the red rock formations, and drove out to Jerome to visit some of the galleries. The last night was cold, rainy, and windy. On the drive back to Phoenix, we saw that the mountain peaks had gotten some snow.

I wanted to visit the Desert Botanical Garden, as there was a Chihuly exhibit going on, so we drove around in circles, trying to find our way to the Garden with our abbreviated map of Phoenix. We finally found it only to discover the exhibit had sold out. It's probably a good idea to schedule these things in advance.

Back in Tucson, I drove Hal to Amado to pick up his RV, and our two rigs headed off to LOW-Hi Ranch in Deming.

I knew Hal liked being with his friends, two of them heavy drinkers. I worried about that but tried to keep my mouth shut. I wasn't always successful.

It was windy and dusty (as usual) in Deming, so a week later, we headed out of there, and set off to visit a few of the state parks. I bought an annual pass for $225. For the next 12 months, I would be able to stay in any of the New Mexico state parks for no charge (or $4/night if I wanted electric).

We spent two nights at Caballo Lake State Park near Truth or Consequences. Our site had a view of the Caballo Mountains across the lake formed by a dam across the Rio Grande. It was quiet and dark at night; the skies were full of stars.

Next was Manzano Mountain State Park near Albuquerque for two nights. This campground is at 7,500 feet, surrounded by Ponderosa pines and alligator juniper. I saw a pair of bright and elegant Stellar's jays flitting about, also a couple of spotted towhees.

On the 24th, we drove 110 miles to the almost new Buffalo Thunder Casino, a little north of Santa Fe, where we camped for ten days.

While camped at the Casino, we took trips to Taos and the Rio Grande Gorge, Los Alamos, and Bandelier National Monument, and we spent an afternoon at the Santa Fe Indian Market.

We drove out along the Chama River to Abiquiu and Ghost Ranch, where we walked the labyrinth. There's something mysterious at Ghost Ranch that pulls at me. I found it easy to understand Georgia O'Keeffe's fascination with the area. I spent some peaceful moments sitting on a bench watching a pair of ravens soaring high along the cliff, their shadows below them on the face of the rock.

Twice we visited the nearby Wildlife Center, the only licensed wildlife vet in New Mexico. The Center had pygmy owls, eastern screech owls, a peregrine falcon, bobcats, and foxes—all of them with injuries that prevented their return to the wild.

I loved this part of New Mexico and planned to come back to spend more time. I wanted to spend a few days camping at Bandelier and make another visit to Los Alamos. Where did they set off the bomb?

In early May, we drove to Las Vegas, New Mexico, to Storrie Lake State Park. It was a windy day, and I watched windsurfers flying across the lake, like one-winged butterflies. Every so often, a gust of wind would tip one over.

On the 6th, we traveled 222 miles to Pueblo, Colorado, and on the 7th, another 212 to Cheyenne, Wyoming. Once we were into Colorado, there was a definite division in the landscape. All the mountains were to our west, topped with snow. The Great Plains were to our east, pale ochre fields stretching up and away to meet the sky, with little vegetation tall enough to obstruct the view.

On May 8th, we took US-85 across southeast Wyoming. The land was flat and unremarkable. A savage wind beat at us from the west. Young tumbleweeds scurried and bounced across the highway in front of me, their more mature counterparts pressed against the fence to my right. Fat-bellied cumulus clouds filled the sky, their lower edges blurred and bleeding into gauzy veils of gray and white near the horizon. When we arrived at BJ's RV park in Lusk, we discovered those veils of moisture contained a mixture of rain, snow, and sleet.

On the 9th, we crossed into South Dakota and the Black Hills and settled again at Hart Ranch in Rapid City. The leaves were opening out on the trees, and the weather couldn't make up its mind. We experienced the first hot day, about 85 degrees, but there was a breeze, so it wasn't uncomfortable. There was always a *breeze* at Hart Ranch. A few days earlier, there had been gusts to 60 mph. We'd stay until early June, then head off to Minnesota to fish.

The weather was chilly. There was rain, and a couple of storms produced pea/marble-sized hail. There's nothing quite like the din of hail striking the roof of your motorhome.

Bijou got out one evening. She disappeared for a bit, then I found her, managed to get hold of her and brought her back. But as I was reaching to open the door, she leaped out of my arms and ran to the other side of Hal's rig. He was away, so I left his screen door open and brought my dinner over to his RV to eat. That way, I could keep an eye on Bijou, where she was hanging out under another rig. Soon, something spooked her, and she came running in.

Hal came back, and we chatted, played cards, and hung out, patting Bijou when she came near, then finally decided to try getting her back to Mehitabel. He picked her up, she went berserk and chomped on his left hand. She howled and growled, but he managed to hold onto her and got her home to me.

We bandaged him up after washing and anointing his wounds. He went back to his rig to sleep. I didn't sleep well. Bijou slept next to my feet, and I steered clear of her when I got up to pee.

Hal didn't feel well all the next day, so the following morning, I insisted we go to the emergency room and get some antibiotics. There we learned that animal bites must be reported, so we waited until a cop came for information that he forwarded to Animal Control. That was unexpected and made me nervous, but no one came to take Bijou and me to jail, and Hal was feeling much better after three days on the antibiotic.

··· 11 ···

Here, There, Everywhere, Hustling

I haven't been everywhere,
but it's on my list. — Susan Sontag

FROM RAPID CITY, we traveled onward to southern Minnesota, and in July, we took off in Mehitabel to visit various Minnesota state parks.

At Itasca State Park, we waded across the source of the mighty Mississippi River. Late one afternoon, we rented a double-seat kayak, paddled the Rum River, and admired a young buck browsing at the water's edge. There were tiny white flowers with stems so threadlike they appeared to be floating above the water.

At Mille Lacs Kathio State Park, there were deer, so elegant with their narrow heads and slender legs, their summer coats a rich red-brown. On a walk one morning, we saw a doe nursing her twin fawns right next to the road

One night we went on a fishing launch on Lake Mille Lacs, and Hal caught two big walleye. No one else got more than one, so they gave us their catch. The captain filleted them all for us, and we had a yummy fish dinner the next night.

Next was Bemidji State Park, where we admired Paul Bunyan and his baby blue ox. I walked the Bog Walk trail after dinner one night and saw delicate clusters of pink lady slippers.

We fished at Bear Head Lake State Park south of Ely; we fished at the foot of Kawishiwi Falls in Ely; we tried fishing from the massive rocks at the edge of Lake Superior at Temperance River State Park; and at Jay Cooke State Park, south of Duluth, we fished in the St. Louis River. No luck anywhere. Our timing was off this year, but it was fun. It is hypnotic watching the bobber and foam swirling in the water.

From Ely, we went north to visit Judge Magney State Park on the North Shore. We had a fantastic dinner at Naniboujou Restaurant and, the next morning, hiked to the Devil's Kettle on the Brule River. Our calves ached from all the stairs. We also walked along the Temperance River—more stairs—on our way south.

We stayed at the casino in Hinckley and partook of their buffet. I swore that was the last buffet I would go to. There's too much mass-produced, not-very-good food. The best part is always the dessert.

Back to southern Minnesota for a couple of weeks. I had a dirt skirt installed on Mehitabel, took her in for an oil change, and we organized supplies and our belongings, getting ready for our long-planned trip north in one rig.

On August 5, we started on our grand adventure, spent one quiet, peaceful night at a Walmart in Ladysmith, Wisconsin, then headed north to Marquette, Michigan, on the Upper Peninsula.

After a couple of nights at an RV park, we moved over to the Ojibwa Casino. There were free electric hookups for RVs, so we remained for another three days and continued to explore the Upper Peninsula by car. One day we went all the way out to Copper Harbor on the Keweenaw Peninsula. It was lovely out there, but so isolated. The 48-year average for snowfall is 240.9 inches. No thanks!

From Marquette, we moved on to Keewadin Shores Casino for a couple of nights and took the hydro-jet ferry out to Mackinac Island.
Only emergency vehi-
cles are allowed on
the island. Residents
get around on foot or
bikes, while tourists
(that would be us) tour
the island in carriages
pulled by big Belgian
and Percheron draft
horses.

There are lots of horses and bicycles, and a strong smell of horse urine wherever you go. The odor surprised me, but the streets are paved, so the urine just sits or goes into the storm drains, rather than soaking into the earth. The town is delightful—famous for its fudge, which was delicious—with lovely homes and hotels along the bay and up on the bluff.

Leaving Keewadin Shores, we headed to Port Huron, where it took almost two hours to get through customs and cross the bridge into Ontario on our way to Niagara Falls. Our day at the Falls was hot and steamy. We did lots of walking and standing in line and got wet from the spray, which felt divine. Neither of us had ever been here before. Did you know that the Niagara River flows north from Lake Erie into Lake Ontario? For some reason, I assumed the river ran south. Oh well, I'm often surprised by geographical realities.

From Niagara, we crossed the Peace Bridge into Buffalo, continued east to Syracuse, then turned north and spent the night in Parish, New York, a town that doesn't appear to have a lot going on in the way of entertainment. There was a small circular dirt track beside the road as we neared the RV park. A big sign in front proclaimed *Lawnmower Races.* Sadly, we didn't stay in the area long enough to witness one.

The next day, we traveled along the St. Lawrence Seaway to Massena, where we spent a few days at Robert Moses State Park, near Dwight D. Eisenhower Lock, the first of four locks on the Seaway. I went to the lock one day and watched a Canadian ship, 740 feet long and loaded with salt, enter the lock, and get lowered 42 feet for the next leg of its journey.

From Massena, we continued across upper New York State, glimpsing the Adirondacks in the distance. We took US-2 right down the middle of Lake Champlain in Vermont, then east through the Green Mountains to St. Johnsbury, where we spent a night camped next to the gurgling Moose River.

The next morning, we proceeded on US-2 through the White Mountains, across New Hampshire (which is narrow at this point), then into Maine. The road followed the Androscoggin River, then the Kennebec (I think), through Rumford, Farmington, and Skowhegan, to Newport, where we camped overnight at a Walmart. The following day, we headed north up I-95 to Houlton, Maine, and crossed the border into New Brunswick, Canada. That night we camped near Fredericton, with a view of the broad St. John River.

On August 22, we drove across New Brunswick to Prince Edward Island. According to the weather reports, Hurricane Bill was heading there as well. CH-2, the main highway across that part of New Brunswick, has many long slow climbs uphill, dark green spruce forests stretching off on both sides.

There were supposed to be lots of moose in the area, but the only ones we saw were on the *Moose Crossing* signs. We did see several roadkill porcupines.

We crossed the Northumberland Strait on the 8.75-mile-long Confederation Bridge and made camp at Pine Hills RV Camp about 15 miles from Charlottetown. That evening we drove into town to Lobster on the Wharf for a yummy lobster dinner, Hal's first experience with that crustacean.

During the last half of the drive to Prince Edward Island, the winds had been gusty. The rain started around eight the next morning, but it was sporadic, so we went into town and walked around the North River/Charlottetown harbor area and Victoria Park. Back to Lobster on the Wharf for lunch and a glass of wine and, as the rain was getting steadier, we headed to camp.

The next morning, we followed the East Coastal Drive of the island. It was overcast, with intermittent rain. We had a great lunch at Rick's Fish & Chips & Seafood in St. Peters, then decided to do the 2.5-mile walk on the Greenwich Dunes Trail in Prince Edward Island National Park. Of course, it immediately started raining steadily, and we got soaked, but it was a lovely walk anyway.

Continuing our drive, we stopped at the Prince Edward Distillery to taste their wild blueberry vodka. Yuck! They had a recipe for a Maritime something-or-other, which called for their vodka mixed with blueberry juice and tonic. That sounded good, but we didn't buy any of the vodka, so we were unable to try it.

On the morning of the 25th, we drove into town, wandered Victoria Row, came back for lunch, then hit the road again, on our way to Nova Scotia.

The little we did see of Prince Edward Island was quite lovely, with goldenrod and Queen Anne's lace everywhere, green fields of potatoes and golden fields covered with giant rolls of hay, so colorful against the rich terra-cotta earth.

After a night at a campground in Glenholme, Nova Scotia, we went to Baddeck Cabot Trail RV Park on Cape Breton Island. The next day, we took the car and made the 180-mile circle drive of Cabot Trail. There were incredible views of St. Lawrence Bay on the west side and the Atlantic on the east, as well as cliffs and maritime forests. It was overcast and windy, but no rain.

On the 28th, we had a beautiful day at last. We wandered around Baddeck Harbor in the afternoon and had pizza at the Yellow Cello that evening with a couple we'd met in the RV park. They were traveling in a new 35-foot RV and were heading to Newfoundland in a couple of days via ferry. Yikes! The thought of putting Mehitabel on a boat to Nova Scotia had struck fear in my heart; to avoid it, I'd added a few hundred miles to our trip, but they'd put their rig on ferries before with no problems. They had spent three weeks in Prince Edward Island and planned a similar amount of time in Newfoundland.

I started to believe that we were moving too often, and we weren't learning as much about each place as I would have liked. I'm not sure why we were in such a rush; we didn't have any deadlines. This country is so vast and so beautiful. We wanted to see it all, but in trying to do that, we were only skimming the surface.

Rushing too much or not, at this point, we were both looking forward to getting back to the states. Canada was more expensive than we had anticipated: gas was costing the equivalent of $3.98/gal, and there was a 13% tax added onto most everything. I discovered to my dismay that my wireless internet connection had sent my phone bill skyrocketing. We spent a windy and rainy night at a Walmart in Truro, then another in St. John, where tropical storm Danny had flooded many of the streets. On the 29th, we headed back toward Maine.

••• 12 •••

The Great Fish Story

I regret less the road not taken than my all-fired hurry
along the road I took. — Robert Brault

BACK ON U.S. soil, we headed for Mount Desert Island and
Bar Harbor, Maine, for some gorgeous weather.

The delightful town of Bar Harbor is located at the
edge of the sea and surrounded by Acadia National Park.
Exploring the park, we clambered over rocks to enjoy the
incredible views. From the summit of Cadillac Mountain, we
saw an enormous cruise ship below in the harbor, looking
like something from outer space, little motor-and-sail boats
all around it.

On our last night, we took a sunset cruise on the Margaret
Todd, a four-mast schooner with lovely sails a beautiful rust
color. Back in the days of cotton sails, rot was a problem, and
sails would be soaked in tannins from tree bark to protect
them from mold and mildew. The resulting color was called

Tanbark. These days sails are made of dacron and are available in two colors: white and Tanbark. It was a thrill to watch those great sails hoisted up and filling with wind, thrumming as the breeze picked up and we flew across the bay.

If you get to Bar Harbor, be sure to try a Wild Blackberry Disaster ice cream cone. It's indescribably delicious. I forget where we got it, but it's well worth your trouble to search for it.

On September 3, we left the area, heading to Portsmouth, New Hampshire, where we stayed at a Walmart. I had tracked down some friends on the internet and discovered one was visiting her son in Portsmouth, so we met for breakfast the next morning. We hadn't seen each other for 20-odd years. It's such a treat to have time to find old friends from far away, and I especially enjoyed seeing and spending time with both old and new friends. All this togetherness in a small space with Hal was beginning to make me feel restless and irritable. It was kind of like wearing clothes that were one size too small.

On September 4, we arrived in Nashua, New Hampshire, where my son Brian lived. The next nine nights, we parked at a quiet neighborhood Walmart, a few miles from his house.

On Labor Day, we joined Brian, his three-year-old son James—my grandson—and his dad John (yes, that would be my ex-husband) to go tuna fishing 30 miles out in the Gulf of Maine on John's classy boat. Hal found the situation strange and kept asking, "Are you still attracted to John?"

We caught some mackerel to use as bait and started looking for tuna. Around two, about to pull up lines and try another spot, Brian hooked one, and the fight was on. The mighty battle lasted a good 90 minutes. My heart was pounding from fear that Brian was going to get pulled overboard. The fish came to the surface once near the end. It was about seven feet long and must have weighed 200 pounds, so the tuna and Brian were a good match. It outsmarted him in the end, diving under the boat and breaking the line on the keel. Three men stood, wide-eyed and silent for about 40 seconds, their mouths hanging open in utter disbelief. I should have gotten a photo!

We drove up to Concord, New Hampshire, to meet my grand-daughter Heather for lunch, after which we continued to Strafford, to spend a few hours with another re-discovered old friend and her husband, at their mini-farm in the woods.

I visited with my dad one afternoon, then stopped for dinner with my friend Ellie and her husband on the way back. Hal hadn't been feeling well for a few days, so he stayed behind.

On the 13th, we moved Mehitabel down to Minuteman RV Park in Littleton, Massachusetts, and drove out to Rutland to see the rest of my family: brothers Steve and Jonathan; sister-in-law Annemarie; and nieces Heather and Jessica. We had a great visit with everyone then headed back to Littleton.

The following day, we picked up my granddaughter Brianna, took a hike in the woods with her and brought her back to the camp for dinner with us before taking her home.

On September 15, we left Littleton and headed for North Carolina. We got wrong online directions to a Walmart in Newburgh, New York, and traveled several miles on a quiet country road before realizing something was wrong. I saw a left turn ahead and thought there was enough room for me to make a U-turn. Wrong! I ended up jack-knifed across the road and, of course, couldn't back up. There I was, hot, sweaty, and rattled, blocking traffic in both directions. Hal and the owner of the house (whose lawn I would have driven over had there not been iron stakes along the edge) got the car unhooked from Mehitabel so I could get her out of the way and headed in the right direction. He then helped Hal get the car hooked up again and gave us instructions to find the Walmart. The iron stakes suggested I was not the first to attempt a U-turn at that spot.

The next morning, we headed south, through the Delaware Water Gap, to Stroudsburg, then on to a Walmart in Allentown, Pennsylvania. There were scattered areas of fall color. We saw a bald eagle with a rabbit in its talons, flying low at about 35 mph.

We drove through Amish country in Lancaster the following day, then onward to Ashland, Virginia, and another Walmart. There were lots of trucks leaving the lot about three-thirty in the morning, and I had trouble sleeping. I started worrying about getting Bijou declawed, which Hal kept asking me to do. I had an appointment with my former vet to check her out, but she was pretty congested, and I was concerned about anesthesia. Finally, we got up and hit the road. In the early afternoon, we arrived at Holly Point on Falls Lake in Raleigh.

Over the next few days, we did errands and shopping and visited with some of my friends. The following week was full of gloomy, dismal weather during which we went to a few movies.

On the 25th, Hal flew back to Minnesota to go bow-hunting for deer, do some fishing, and pick up his rig. I stayed to deal with doctor, dentist, and vet appointments, get a haircut and take care of Mehitabel's needs before making the long trek west.

I was at the park on Falls Lake for another ten days, then moved out to Zebulon, east of Raleigh, to camp on a small farm owned by my hairdresser and her builder husband.

What a fantastic setup I had there. I was plugged into electricity at his office, had access to a bathroom with a shower, a view of ducks on a pond, two beautiful horses, and a sheep named Isabel.

One morning I looked up from my computer to see the horses galloping across the pasture. They looked so proud and full of joy, their heads up and tails lifted high, with Isabel doing her best to keep up. Another ghostly, foggy morning, there was an enormous flock of Canada Geese in the pasture; they fed for a time, then took to the air with much squawking and wheeled about to come in for a landing again. Dozens of birds were all acting with one mind. How did they do it?

When I stepped outside the rig, I could hear a rooster across the street, cock-a-doodle-doing so hard it was a wonder he had a voice left. He crowed all day long, perhaps because the days were overcast, and he was trying to make the sun come up.

I was working on my website, updating prices, and adding a few products. It turned out that the several microsites I had ordered some time ago were not even up. I sent off an email to the company and lodged a formal complaint to the Arizona Better Business Bureau, but knew I was unlikely to get my money back. The company now had a grade of *F*. I decided to shut down the bird product site when I got back to New Mexico. It would be a relief. I'd learned a lot, but wasted a lot of money. If I put that time into my painting and writing, who knows what might happen?

I got my doctor and dentist appointments out of the way and took Bijou to the vet. Due to her congestion, the vet did not want to anesthetize her, so no declawing, which was a relief. I had work done on Mehitabel and visited with several friends one more time. It was such a treat to have women friends to talk with again. I had truly missed that.

On October 17, I started the long trek on I-40 across half the U.S., overnighted at my favorite welcome center in Tennessee the first night, then at Walmarts in West Nashville, Lonoke, Arkansas, and Checotah, Oklahoma.

On October 21, at the end of a terrible drive with rain and blustery winds, I met Hal at Foss Lake State Park in Oklahoma, a lovely park next to a reservoir with lots of geese and funny little water birds called coots. He hadn't gotten any hunting or fishing done, as the weather in Minnesota had been cold and rainy. He had wrecked the cab-over on his RV, driving into a Walmart lot with an arm over the entrance to keep out big rigs. His RV was just a little too tall. He was not a happy camper and wanted to take it to get repaired in Albuquerque, New Mexico. He thought I should follow him there. We were heading in that direction anyway, to Santa Rosa Lake State Park, so I suggested that he take his rig to Albuquerque from there, then come back with his car to join me until the repairs were complete. He finally agreed that it didn't make sense for us to sit around in Albuquerque.

The next day we arrived in New Mexico, land of (almost) eternal sunshine, where we camped at the park for the next couple of weeks. Hal took his RV to Camping World in Albuquerque, then came back.

The first week was chilly, but then things warmed up, and the sun shone daily.

The lake was a cloudy tan color with blasted, sun-whitened juniper skeletons along the edges. It was an almost colorless palette, only shades of beige with random splotches of small green, ground-hugging plants. On the higher trails, slabs of shale or sandstone looked like petrified beaches. All this land was once at the bottom of an ocean.

Santa Rosa is a small town with only one little market and a lot of boarded-up businesses. Old Route 66 goes right through the middle of it, but I-40 put an end to the traffic those businesses used to enjoy.

We explored the area, driving down to Fort Sumner to visit Billy the Kid's gravesite one day, to Las Vegas to raid the nearest Walmart on another day. On a third day, we explored the desert on a gravel road out of Puerto de Luna and got lost. The cottonwoods along the Pecos River were all turning golden.

We had an awful falling-out on our Las Vegas Walmart trip. Hal tended to keep at me when grocery shopping. "Look at this. Don't we need these? Come down this aisle." Asking him to please stop didn't work. It drove me crazy as I had a list and was also trying to think of other things we needed. I liked to get through shopping as fast as possible. Plus, I was hungry, which makes me impatient and crabby.

When we got back, he packed up all his stuff and left to spend the next two nights at a motel. He came by in the morning, we did some walking and talking, and things got straightened out. He takes my irritability and crabbiness so personally, and his already low self-esteem dives. There's no question I need to learn to relax and not be so irritable. But the whole episode seemed kind of staged to me—like he deliberately kept pushing until I snapped—and it left me with an uncomfortable feeling. Relationships are stressful. I felt like I needed to do things with him, but there were so many times I just wanted to be left alone. Hal didn't seem to have enough interests to keep him occupied.

We played cards and had dinner, and he left for the motel. He was back the next morning, fixed a couple of things, and went to get the RV. He decided to head straight down to Deming from there and said he might drive the car back to meet me somewhere down the road. Maybe he triggered the blowup so he'd have a reason to go to Deming. I would enjoy the time alone but knew I'd miss him.

I got out the generator manual and learned how to change the air filter. I ended up filthy and cut my finger, but got the job done. There were times I amazed myself.

··· 13 ···

GPS Recalculating

You have powers you never dreamed of. You can do things you never thought you could do. There are no limitations in what you can do except the limitations of your own mind.
— Darwin Kingsley

I TRAVELED SOUTH along the Pecos River the following morning to Bottomless Lakes State Park, outside of Roswell. The bottomless lakes are a chain of eight sinkholes, 17 to 90 feet deep, formed as circulating water dissolves salt and gypsum deposits to create subterranean caverns. Eventually, the roofs of the caverns collapse, and the sinkholes soon fill with water.

I parked alongside the bluff next to Lea Lake in the tent area. Next to me was a man from Iowa camping in a small tent with his dog. On the other side of him was a young couple, car-camping with their dog. Bathrooms with showers were nearby.

The late afternoon sun and feathery cirrus clouds were dreamy, and there were sunspots on both sides of the sun, making little rainbows.

I met Linda and Ron, a pleasant couple with an enormous Prévost on the other side of the lake. They had a trailer in tow that was almost as large because Ron was in the process of refurbishing the interior of the customized bus; the trailer carried all his tools and supplies.

Linda and I went into Roswell for lunch and a visit with the Aliens at the Visitor Center. The next day, I went back to town to the Art Center and the Convention Center. Roswell is a fascinating town, famous for an alleged UFO crash and U.S. Army/Air Force cover-up back in 1947. I visited the UFO Museum to learn more and ended up becoming a believer.

On the way home, I stopped at the Bitter Lake Wildlife Refuge, winter home to thousands of sandhill cranes and snow geese. Every time I got out of the car, I heard the swelling sound of birds chattering to each other.

Hal drove over on the 11th to join me, and everything was glorious. I couldn't believe how different I felt; what a world of difference in me if I have some time alone.

On the 13th, we moved down to Brantley Lake State Park, (another dam on the Pecos River) 12 miles north of Carlsbad. The ranger told us there used to be fishing, but now there was a ban on eating the fish due to a high concentration of DDT. That was bad enough, but every winter, they were also getting a

blue-green alga that killed everything. I often wonder what we are doing to our world.

We visited Sitting Bull Falls Recreation Area in Lincoln National Forest, wandered below the 150-foot falls, then hiked to the top on a steep and strenuous path. Here, and at Bottomless Lakes, the surface of the rocks is rough and sharp, like coral. I often wished I had taken a geology course in college, though I would likely have forgotten it all by now.

Another day we went to Carlsbad Caverns and descended 754-feet on a mile-long paved walkway into the depths of the cavern. The walk down was steep; my toes pushed against the fronts of my sneakers. By the time we got to the bottom, sharp pains were shooting across my right knee. But it was well worth the effort, and, happily, there was an elevator to get us back up. Imagine the work that went into exploring that labyrinth and constructing the walkways.

The nights were getting cold; Hal was concerned about his rig freezing in Deming, so he left on the 18th to drive back. I packed up and headed out the next morning, north to Artesia, then west on 82, winding through the Sacramento Mountains, following a little river through a valley between the hills and cliffs.

The fields of dried grasses echoed the soft ochre of the rocky cliffs. Many of the Cottonwoods were already bare, but some large ones still had leaves of such a pale tan they sparkled white and silver in the sun.

The road climbed gradually, ending at over 8,000 feet in Cloudcroft. The descent was considerably more abrupt, down through High Rolls, then down again to Alamogordo. At several points, I caught glimpses of White Sands, like a field of snow, in the distance.

On to Alamogordo, then Las Cruces, where I connected with I-10 to Deming, arriving mid-afternoon at the LoW-Hi RV Ranch, feeling shaky and stiff. I'd spent too long sitting and needed to eat. I called Hal when I was a few minutes away; he showed up when I was on the roof, putting up the solar panel. I was hot, dirty, and tired, and he looked as though he'd had a few beers.

I escaped for a half-hour to put my house in order and sit for a few minutes with my drink, then he came over, had a couple more beers, and started another at dinner. He is different when he drinks, and I don't like being with him. We spent the night apart after I told him the main reason I didn't like being at LoW-Hi was that he drinks more, which was not healthy for him, or our relationship.

Since we had two RVs, I requested time alone each morning and used it to put on a quiet CD and do my yoga. I'd been doing it for the past few weeks and enjoyed it. It's a good way to start the day.

My internal GPS was acting up, *recalculating*. More and more, I felt like this part of my life wasn't working too well, and maybe I needed to change direction. I needed to get some distance and see if I could decide what to do.

One gorgeous afternoon, I drove up to City of Rocks State Park alone. Sculpted by wind and rain, the brown, gray and ochre rocks stand, sometimes alone like a warning outpost. In other spots, they appear to be leaning together in a huddle, like frightened old women with sagging breasts and bellies, billowing hips. It's a fantastic, beautiful, mysterious place. But that day, at least, it didn't help me find any answers.

The weather changed, and on November 30, we fled cold, windy, rainy weather with the threat of snow in Deming, and high-tailed it to Casino del Sol in Tucson, where the sun was shining, and temperatures were a bit warmer.

We parked in one of the Casino's outer lots; there were lights at regular intervals, so the area was quite bright. I looked out the window one night and saw a small herd of javelinas trotting across the lot.

We decided to stay for a bit before heading on to Quartzsite and Yuma. We planned to spend a month in Yuma, then return to Tucson.

Well, so much for plans. Life has a way of throwing you a curve occasionally.

———◦◦◦———

Hal's stomach had been bothering him, and he was short of breath at times, so he finally agreed to see a non-VA doctor on December 7th. The doctor examined him thoroughly and recommended a stress test which he had on the 10th.

There were several doctors in his room when the test was over; they expressed concern about a possible blockage in one or more arteries, so he scheduled a cardiac catheterization. The result of that was not good. They told us he needed a triple bypass as soon as possible.

During the two weeks before surgery, we moved from the Casino parking lot into an RV park, putting his RV in storage and living in Mehitabel, with full hookups. Doctors suggested an RV wasn't the best place for him to stage his recovery, so we looked at apartments. We found one we liked, but Hal wanted to check with VA to see if they had other options. I tried to stay calm, but it felt like my life was suddenly spiraling out of control. I'm sure he felt the same. I was close to tears and frustrated that we couldn't just make a decision and move forward. I needed to deal with renting the furniture and moving all the kitchen stuff, housewares, and clothes while he was in the hospital. I was worried about him; the doctors wanted him to start on a statin drug without even knowing his cholesterol level. Hal was like my mother in that regard. Whatever the doctor said was bound to be right. The whole thing was overwhelming; I felt as though I were pushing through molasses or thick fog. Never would I submit to an operation like that and all those drugs without trying a more natural, holistic approach first.

Finally, we agreed on an apartment and arranged to rent furniture.

On the 28th, he had surgery at the VA Hospital—a double bypass only, as the third artery apparently wasn't blocked too severely. Either that or the doctor was tired.

The following week, while Hal was in the hospital, was about the worst I'd ever had. The second day after surgery, he had a full-blown anxiety attack and left me five messages during the night, demanding that I bring him his medications. I did that in the morning, but the medical staff wouldn't let him have his pills. I spent most of that day at the hospital, listening to his constant mutterings about the *animals* and how they were mistreating him. It's like there was a monster inhabiting his body. He refused medication from any of them though he finally took an anti-anxiety pill from me. If I tried to talk to him, he shushed me and sent me to my corner so he could rest.

"I'll leave here and drive off in my RV. Forget the apartment; I can get better all by myself."

When I held his hand, he was unresponsive, and his eyes were dead and cold. He was hateful to everyone. It sure wouldn't have taken much to convince me to take off for Quartzsite on my own the next day. I kept telling myself that it wasn't Hal talking; it was the meds and the surgery. Poor Bijou; she must have wondered why I was sobbing and wailing that evening. Thank heaven for her warm, loving presence.

Hal was himself the next day, and the recovery started, though it was halting, as his anxiety attack had taken a toll. He seemed most happy that the surgeon allowed him to have a beer with lunch each day.

I got the lease signed, making sure I could cancel it in the event of a medical emergency. Then I drove back and forth between our RVs and the apartment, moving our clothes, dishes, pots and pans, food, and TVs. On the 3rd, I helped him escape from the hospital. He wanted me to take him straight to the Casino. I refused, which brought on a nasty remark or two. We went to Mehitabel for one night, met the furniture folks the next morning at the apartment and moved in, though I still had several trips to make.

The last trip was Bijou and her litter box.

Part 3

MAINTAIN YOUR ENVIRONMENT (2010)

··· 14 ···

Recovery

It is not the strongest of the species that survive, nor the most intelligent, but the one most responsive to change.
— Charles Darwin

HAL WASN'T ALLOWED to drive for six weeks. He had to ride in the back seat with a pillow between the shoulder harness and his chest. He didn't like that at all. I should have worn a uniform and cap so they would think him someone important.

I was feeling strung out doing all the shopping, cooking, and cleaning, plus he wanted to go somewhere almost every day. Getting up early and doing yoga helped to get my days off to a good start.

We had a two-bedroom apartment, and the rental furniture was comfortable. There was an L-shaped arrangement of sofa and love seat in the living room with a big square coffee table. I'd brought over a few of my favorite books and had them piled on a corner of the table near where I sat. One day I returned from grocery shopping to discover Hal had taken my books off the table. When I asked about them, he pointed to the floor next to the TV, saying, "I think the table looks much better with nothing on it."

That was odd; at least I thought so. I kept my mouth shut, however, and took a few of the books into the second bedroom, which was my office, and put the rest of them back on the table. Hal left them alone after that.

Once my tour of duty as a chauffeur was over, I escaped the apartment a couple of times a week by signing up for classes in Spanish, drawing, and watercolor. Tucson offers so much in the arts, and I loved it. I had thought Hal might be interested in the Spanish course and offered to take it over again with him, but he didn't want to.

Hal wasn't happy about the art classes. More than once, he said, "Your painting is good already. You don't need to take classes."

I held my ground, however. "I've always done my best painting either during or right after a workshop. I learn a lot and love being with other artists."

I don't know how well we would have survived in the RV during this. It was nice to have room to spread out a little. There were places to walk nearby; Hal did a lot of that, and I joined him several times a week.

I was working on a new website. This one would be all about RVing since that was what I was doing. I'd done some research and decided on a hosting company. Having learned from my earlier experience, I knew better than to spend a lot of money upfront; this company had a reasonable annual fee. The work was going slowly, however, as I got so little uninterrupted time, and the internet connection was not great.

One afternoon a big javelina walked right by our patio and trotted down the sidewalk. Another evening, we heard snorting and saw several javelinas, including a little one, rooting around in the dirt next to the patio. They were after the sunflower seeds Hal had been throwing out for the birds. Later I looked out and saw six of them, with two young-sters, coming down the hill. Good heavens, we were living in a wildlife park.

Toward the end of February, we went to the Tucson Rodeo, a significant event in this city; kids even get off school for opening day. It was beautiful weather and lots of fun watching the calf-roping and bronc riding.

On Valentine's Day, we had a picnic and hike at Saguaro National Park. It had rained on several occasions, so the des-ert was starting to turn green. The ocotillos, dead-looking spiny stalks during dry seasons, were now covered with tiny leaves, and many were sporting red flowers. It was exciting to see everything starting to bloom.

I took Bijou to get her teeth cleaned and was going to get her declawed as well, but the vet advised against it. He said the only safe time to do it is at the kitten stage, and he didn't like that idea either. As an adult cat, there would be a longer healing time, risk of infection, and significant stress to her system. He convinced me declawing was no longer an option. I was thankful to have solid reasons for not putting her through that.

Hal was still bringing up Bijou as an obstacle at times. It was so irritating and frustrating. He needed to let go of this obsession. I had been clear from the beginning that I would not get rid of her. There were moments I was ready to walk out the door. Why didn't I? I'm not sure. I was still trying to convince myself that, with more space, we'd be able to work things out, but my arguments were sounding pretty thin. I also felt like I needed to help him get through this recovery period. I was confused as to where my responsibility for his comfort and happiness ended. I'd never been good at creat-ing boundaries in my relationships or my real estate business either. Without limitations, there's a tendency for all my time and energy to get consumed.

We found a realtor and did some looking at houses and townhomes. After a few excursions, we stopped, and should not have started it in the first place. The surgery and recovery were more than enough to deal with, prices were still going down, and interest rates seemed like they would stay down, so we decided to revisit the situation in the fall. We both felt we'd like to winter in Tucson in the future.

On March 6, we drove up to Scottsdale to meet my son Jeff and his family. His seven-year-old son Jack had become an obsessed baseball fan, and Jeff and Laurie had developed an equal passion for the game. They attended almost all the San Francisco Giants home games, and since Scottsdale was the Giants spring training ground, the three of them flew in to see a few games.

The Giants trounced Arizona's Diamondbacks 12 to 6, in an exciting game. Scottsdale was jammed with baseball fans, all having a noisy and happy time after the games.

Hal and I drove down to Tubac in mid-March, had lunch at Shelby's Bistro, and wandered the galleries 'til our feet gave out. It was in the 80s, but there was a breeze. Spring had arrived. Tiny leaves were appearing on the trees, more flowers were blooming, and blossoms on the several varieties of prickly pear and cholla were on the verge of opening up.

Three months after surgery, Hal was healing well. He had started cardiac rehab at two months and was going three times a week. We had the apartment until the end of April. At that point, we'd load up the RVs and start heading north to resume our adventures. At least that was the plan.

Watching the desert come to life in the spring was a joy. Small yellow flowers covered the graceful palo verde and mesquite trees. Prickly pears sported translucent, tender new pads, their edges crowded with buds that opened as pale yellow, pink gold, or bright yellow flowers; cholla blossoms were dark red, pink, orange, or yellow. Giant saguaros had long-necked buds on the tops of all their arms, as well as on the main trunk. Some were starting to open; soon, they would be crowned with white as the profusion of buds burst into bloom.

At the end of April, we moved out of the apartment and rented an 8x5 storage unit. Hal cleaned out his RV and sold it to a dealer in town, then sold his trailer; I emptied some compartments in Mehitabel so there would be more space for him during our summer on the road. Most of what I cleared out went into the storage unit. So, we were down to just one RV. I had mixed feelings about that; he'd made another unilateral decision. I anticipated some difficulties but tried to remain optimistic.

We finally finished bringing the last of our belongings over to my RV, moved it out of storage at Desert Trails RV Park, and turned in the keys at the apartment.

My son Jeff called one afternoon to tell me Laurie had been diagnosed with breast cancer a couple of weeks previously. My eyes filled with tears; she was too young! She would go through chemo, then have a mastectomy. They were staying positive, but I hurt for them and was so afraid Jeff and Jack might lose her. What a horrible disease.

··· 15 ···

Chasing 75 Degrees

Keep close to nature's heart…and break clear away, once in a while, and climb a mountain or spend a week in the woods. Wash your spirit clean. — John Muir

ON MAY 4, we hit the road, heading north to Show Low. It was a long drive through the beautiful desert, then mountain passes. The cliffs and colors between Globe and Show Low were gorgeous. Yucca was blooming on the hills, and patches of Indian paintbrush bloomed on the roadside. The Salt River raced far below us.

The next day we stopped at Painted Desert National Monument on I-40 for lunch, then drove out to Blue Mesa, taking photos of unusual, colorful, geological things along the way. The balance of the drive, north on US-191 up to Chinle, Arizona, was tough, with high winds and lots of big hills. I don't like the winds at all when driving. An RV is tall, and gusts can knock it around, making me tense and anxious.

Although we were down to one rig for this RV adventure, we still had two cars. I drove Mehitabel, towing my Corolla, while Hal drove his vehicle, not willing to leave it behind; I'm not sure why. Maybe he felt it gave him more freedom, more options. The positive side of this was that we never had to unhook and rehook my car since we had his available. The not so positive part was that I had no one to help with the driving.

The Cottonwood Campground at Canyon de Chelly had no fees at all, which had something to do with the fact that all this area is Navajo Reservation land. The canyon is spectacular. The floor of it is some 500-700 feet below brilliant rusty-red cliffs, with a few scattered Navajo farms. A creek lined with vibrant lime green cottonwoods wound through the middle of the canyon. We saw small bands of sheep far below and watched ravens, sleek and glossy, soaring high on the rising currents of warm air.

Dust storms are a regular event in these parts; we drove through one coming into town, and the visibility shrank to about 75 feet. A fine grit soon covered surfaces in the RV. At the campground, we got two radio stations and no TV at all. I never minded going without TV, and Hal was usually able to find a video. I would have liked to read more, but there wasn't much quiet time when he was with me. He either wanted to talk or play his CDs. The nearby Thunderbird Motel had wi-fi, so I was able to connect to the

Internet through that, which was lucky as my wireless card was no use at all.

We packed some sandwiches one day and hiked down to White House Ruins. It took us a half-hour to hike the 500 feet down to the bottom, where we wandered, ate our lunch, and watched kids splashing in the creek. It took a full hour for the hike back up, as we stopped every 50 feet or so to catch our breath. The elevation in this area is about 6000 feet. White House Ruins is the only hike you can do on your own; for all other entries into the canyon, you need a Navajo guide.

The next day we drove about 30 miles south of Chinle to the Navajo rug auction at Hubbell Trading Post in Ganado. My dream was to one day buy one of those beautiful rugs. I especially loved the Two Gray Hills patterns, traditional Navajo weavings blending natural, un-dyed wool in shades of gray, beige, cream, brown, and black. Their intricate designs include a border, four matching corner elements, and a large central full or belted diamond. Hubbell Trading Post has been there for more than 100 years and is the oldest continuously operating trading post in the Navajo Nation.

Our last night at Cottonwood Campground, we became surrounded by Airstream travel trailers, a group gathering. It was neat to see them all.

On May 10, we drove up US-160 to Cortez, Colorado. It wasn't a bad drive, mostly flat, through a bizarre landscape. The red rock rises out of the ground and is carved by wind and rain into weird spires and needles. One looked like an African termite mound.

We spent two nights at Sundance RV Park in Cortez, a lovely park within walking distance to the Colorado Visitor Center, restaurants, and shopping. On the 13th, we moved the ten miles to Mesa Verde National Park, where we spent five days, and guess what? On the second day, the Airstream Group all started coming in. I met the owner of one, who gave me his card, with the slogan, *Chasing 75 degrees*. That could be the mantra for most RVers, come to think of it. This time of year, we continually move further north, or to a higher elevation, to maintain a comfortable temperature. None of us were having much luck with temperatures at present. It was chilly, the park had opened just a couple days before, and there was spitting snow a few times.

We did much driving, and some hiking and puffing while there, saw lots of mule deer, several magpies, and many cliff dwellings; Mesa Verde has some of the most notable and best-preserved ones on our continent. Ancestral Puebloans started building under the overhanging cliffs in the 1190s, after centuries of living on the mesas. They continued to farm up top as they constructed, sometimes one-room storage units, but also villages of 100 rooms or more. By the late 1270s, they started migrating south into Arizona and New Mexico; by 1300, the occupation of Mesa Verde ended.

We drove west about 50 miles one day to Hovenweep National Monument, over the border in Utah. It's a fantastic place, with ruins of square or round towers on the edges of cliffs, surrounded by miles and miles of sagebrush. People started settling here in A.D. 900; by the late 1200s, it was home to over 2,500 people. Those early people were great craftsmen and masons, and some of their work was even more skilled than at Mesa Verde. By 1300, they had moved on, probably forced out by a combination of drought, depleted resources, and warfare. Their descendants and those of the Puebloans at Mesa Verde are present-day Zuni, Hopi, and Pueblo.

It was a lovely day, warm for a change. Taking a different route back, we saw luscious green farmland, with tractors out turning the red soil in some fields, complicated irrigation piping systems watering the green crops in others, and Abajo Peak, covered with snow, in the distance.

We stopped for an early dinner at Nero's in Cortez, and I had the best salmon I'd ever tasted. It was covered with peppercorns, marinated with molasses and orange juice concentrate, resting on a bed of orzo with dried cherries, and covered with wilted spinach. Two glasses of local red wine made it perfect.

On the 16th, we visited the Anasazi Heritage Center, an incredible museum in Dolores. We hiked a half-mile up to a point overlooking MacPhee Lake and the ruins of a pueblo. We saw a myrtle warbler, a black-headed grosbeak, and an eagle soaring over the lake, then a canyon towhee when we got back to camp. Note to self: buy a new bird book. My two were about fifty years old.

The next day we drove 36 miles to a campground in Durango. I loved these short trips; it's tiring driving an RV. The following day we took the car and drove the pass to Silverton, then Red Mountain Pass to Ouray. It was a chilly, overcast day, but a gorgeous drive even so. We had seen the leaves opening during the past week in Cortez and Mesa Verde, but there were no leaves at all on the aspens up in the San Juan Mountains, just bare branches, lots of snow, and huge spruces. We savored delicious chili for lunch at Grumpy's Saloon in Silverton.

A few snowflakes flew around on the way up; more snow and wind as we came back through the pass. I had made this drive by myself in 2001. That had been a white-knuckle journey, with my eyes glued to the road, so I enjoyed being able to look at the view while Hal drove.

We left Durango on the 19th and took US-160 over Wolf Creek Pass (10,850 feet) to a Walmart in Alamosa, a smallish town in the middle of a flat plain surrounded by snow-capped mountains in every direction. Every pasture along the way had at least a few horses grazing.

On the way to Pueblo the next morning, we took a short detour to Great Sand Dunes National Park. Star Dune, at 750', is the tallest in North America. Leaving the park, we continued on US-160, over La Veta Pass (9,413 feet), joined

I-25 in Walsenburg, and overnighted at a KOA campground north of Pueblo.

From Pueblo, we journeyed to Loveland, Colorado, and a Walmart parking lot. I discovered the next morning that I had forgotten to turn the key off Accessory in my car (not the first time that happened, and probably not the last), so my battery was dead. How convenient that we were at Walmart; I went in and bought jumper cables.

May 22 was the most grueling drive of all as we decided to go the full distance to Hart Ranch up in Rapid City, South Dakota—about 360 miles. We took I-25 up to Cheyenne, then east on I-80 to Kimball, Nebraska, then north on NE-71, through Scottsbluff, a lovely area with sculptured sandstone cliffs. There were vicious gusting winds the whole way. We finally reached Hart Ranch in the late afternoon, after 8.5 hours of driving. Way too far to drive an RV in one day.

There must be a better way to get to Rapid City, to say nothing of a better time of year. Last year, about two weeks earlier, we went through Cheyenne, continued north on US-85 to Mule Creek Junction, then headed east on US-18 into South Dakota. It, too, was a horrendously windy, tense, and exhausting drive.

Most of the next day, I spent washing my filthy RV. Hal left for Minnesota to visit with family and take care of some business. I was taking time off traveling for a bit, to catch up on computer work, read, wash and wax the car and RV, and maybe do some painting.

I was working hard on the new website and genuinely enjoying the involvement. I'd pulled together all the email updates I'd sent to my family and friends since starting this adventure and was writing pages about other aspects of RVing. I planned to include affiliate marketing in the hopes that it would someday be a source of income. A few friends had even suggested that I put all my adventures into a book with photos, and I liked that idea.

I hadn't painted yet but had such good intentions.

The weather was typical for Rapid City—warm and humid one day, the next about 20 degrees cooler, cloudy, and windy. When I stopped by the pool, I discovered the heater had died, so the water temperature was dropping.

••• 16 •••

Bighorn Mountains, Glacier National Park

*A good day is when no one shows up and
you don't have to go anywhere.* — Burt Shavitz; Burt's Bees

HAL CAME BACK, and we stayed at Hart Ranch until the
end of June. During that time, we added almost four cubic
feet of storage space to Mehitabel. You may not think this
is a big deal, but when you live in about 280 square feet, it's
beyond exciting to find a way to add a few more.

We removed the overhead TV that came with the rig.
That was not an easy job, but Hal got it out at last. We mea-
sured the resulting space and had some plywood cut at Lowe's
for the bottom and back. Once they were in place, we added
a shelf and had a cabinet door made at a local woodworking
shop. Voila!

I had also bought two drawers from Camping World, which we installed under the dinette table, creating an out-of-sight storage place for all the small items that used to clutter the tabletop.

The park's pool heater stayed broken for the balance of our stay. I swam one morning when the pool temperature was 70 degrees, did ten laps, sat in the hot tub for five minutes, swam another ten minutes, and finished up with a few minutes in the hot tub. It took me about three hours to warm up.

Visiting Bear Country USA, a drive-thru wildlife park in the Black Hills, we saw deer, elk, reindeer, bighorn sheep, mountain goats, and many bears, some of them intent on trying to create new bears. The best part was watching the cubs, in a large area of their own. They were so small, active, and playful. A handler came in with treats for them, and they surrounded her, trying to climb her leg, and bawling to be picked up and held.

There was a rip-roaring thunderstorm, then a tornado warning which kept us awake one night. It felt as though the wind were going under the coach at times; then it would bang down on the roof, then slam into the side. I feared Mehitabel would flip.

We ate dinner one evening at the State Game Lodge in Custer State Park. The structure had served as a summer White House for Calvin Coolidge back in 1927. By the time we finished eating, it was pouring rain. Back in camp, there was a gorgeous double rainbow. All the RVs were shining in the sun, surrounded by black clouds. We stood looking up at the sun breaking through and watched raindrops floating through the sunlight toward us. It felt like we were inside one of those plastic snow globes—a magical moment.

On June 28, we drove to Devils Tower in Wyoming once again. This trip, we got off the interstate and followed SD-34 West, which becomes WY-24. It's a beautiful drive—only a two-lane road, with little traffic—the hills all emerald and lime green. We stayed two nights, dry-camping, and would have liked another day or two, but it was too hot and muggy.

Early one morning, we hiked across prairie dog city, up onto the hills at the base of the tower, then down and across the plain again. The prairie dogs stood tall and still, like little statues, then popped down their holes when we came too close. A couple of young ones ignored us as they nibbled away at some good green stuff. We'd seen so many babies this year: bear cubs, baby pronghorn, colts, fawns, calves, even moose.

On July 1, we arrived at the Bighorn National Forest, where we stayed a week, enjoying the cooler temperatures at 8,200 feet. It was 31 degrees one morning, with a little snow on the ground.

Everything was bright green, with wildflowers blooming here and there. The woods were so pretty, the sunlight streaming down through tall, skinny lodgepole pines onto a carpet of green grass and huckleberry bushes. Hal did some fishing, and we had two delicious dinners of pan-fried trout. There were frequent sightings of deer and moose, and we enjoyed tasty elk burgers at a restaurant for lunch one day.

The last time we drove through Wyoming to Yellowstone, we had taken US-16 over the Powder River Pass in the Bighorn Mountains. This time we were planning to follow 14A down the other side of the mountains. But at the Visitor Center in Burgess Junction, the rangers warned us against taking that route with the RV as there is a 12-mile stretch with a 10 percent grade. A rig had crashed on that road the previous year. Their advice may have saved Bijou and me.

Heeding their warning, we took US-14 down the mountain to Greybull, then US-310 up to Lovell, to Horseshoe Bend Campground in the Bighorn Canyon Recreation Area. The high point of our three-day stay was visiting the Pryor Mountain Mustang Refuge. We saw several groups of these beautiful wild horses, descended from the Spanish Barb and North African Andalusian.

On July 10, we headed for the Ponderosa Campground in Cody, Wyoming. While there, we visited the Buffalo Bill Museum, a complex of three museums. In the Western Art section, we saw terrific Bierstadt, Moran, Remington, and Russell paintings, along with more contemporary painters. On our last night, we went to the Cody Rodeo, which goes on every single night in the summer. It's a great show.

Things had been okay between us for the past several weeks, but we had one of our meltdowns in Cody. I can't remember the reason, and we talked it out the next morning, but I was starting to feel a bit frayed. Too much togetherness probably.

On July 13, we took WY-120, part of the Chief Joseph Scenic Byway, out of Cody and into Montana, where we connected with I-90 West and made our way to Big Timber and the Spring Creek Campground and Trout Ranch. The Wyoming part of the drive was especially lovely with the Beartooth Mountains to the west, hills and sagebrush plains everywhere else. All that beautiful empty, lonely space called to something in my soul and brought tears to my eyes.

This was one of the most beautiful RV parks we'd ever seen. Boulder River ran through it. There were ponds with big rainbow trout, creeks, cottonwoods, green lawns, peace, and quiet. In the distance, we could see the snow-covered Gallatin Range and the Crazy Mountains.

On the 15th, we took off and headed north on US-191, then northwest on US-87 to Great Falls, to spend the night at a Walmart on Smelter Avenue. There was an obnoxious smell there, as we were right across the street from a gas refinery. I bought scads of groceries for our upcoming week in Glacier National Park with the WINs.

It was a beautiful drive the next day, following US-2 along the southern edge of Glacier National Park and the Middle Fork of the Flathead River, to Emery Bay Group Campground, in Flathead National Forest. We drove the final four miles on an incredibly dusty gravel road. The campsite was a mess. Of the two loops in the group area, the WINs had reserved Loop A, but it was full, so we went over to Loop B, which was holding the overflow. An assortment of towed or towing vehicles was parked helter-skelter, all coated with a thick layer of dust. We took the last spot.

On Saturday, we took a forestry road up to Desert Mountain, winding up and around and up again. At the top, we found terrific views in every direction, snow-covered mountains, the Hungry Horse reservoir way below. On the way down, we saw a mountain lion. It trotted across the road and disappeared into the woods. That was pretty exciting!

After a delicious potluck breakfast with the WINs on Sunday, we moved to an RV park on the main road in Hungry Horse, thus eliminating the drive back and forth on that four-mile stretch of dusty road.

We spent the whole of one glorious day in the park, driving the Going-to-the-Sun-Road. There were broken clouds, occasional sprinkles, and incredible views: waterfalls, wildflowers, snow-covered mountains in every direction, deep

valleys hanging between the peaks, scooped out by long-ago glaciers. It was, by far, the most beautiful park we'd ever seen.

At Logan Pass, the summit, we hiked part of the Hidden Lake Trail, but the altitude (about 6,600 feet) got to Hal, and the second half of the trail was snow-covered, so we didn't go all the way. We saw bighorn sheep in the distance, a hoary marmot, and many Colombian ground squirrels.

Leaving Logan Pass, we started down the east side. On the retaining wall, posing as if he were paid $500/day to do so, was a handsome bighorn. He stood calmly, looking at us, or admiring the distant view, as car after car paused to take photos.

When we reached Rising Sun, we stopped at Two Dog Flat and joined several WINs for lunch, then started the return trip. Two bighorns rested near the road at Logan Pass, and beyond them was a mountain goat and her kid.

Our last morning, we took a rafting trip on the Middle Fork of the Flathead River. The rivers are all a beautiful aqua, crystal clear and cold.

••• 17 •••

More Rumblings From My GPS

Figure out what you're passionate about. If you're not passionate about something, go find it. We do not need more unengaged boring people to inhabit this planet.
— Ben Heppner

LEAVING GLACIER NATIONAL Park, we proceeded to Hamilton, Montana, for a visit with my childhood friend, Nancy, and her husband, Ron. They own land with a large barn and spend time camping there every summer. It had been close to twenty years since I'd last seen Nancy, and it was fantastic having a chance to catch up with her. We talked and talked: family, relationships, aging, health, and life in general.

A canal runs through their meadow, and the current was perfect; by swimming hard, you could stay in one place. That's like life, come to think of it. Evenings we shared dinner at a table under a big beach umbrella next to the canal. It was so peaceful watching the sun drop behind the Bitterroot Range, the swallows swooping over the water, and dragonflies glittering in the sun like turquoise needles.

Leaving Hamilton, we drove over Lolo Pass into Idaho and stayed at a National Forest campground on the Lochsa River. It was a beautiful spot, with giant moss-draped spruces and cedars, tree-covered mountains in every direction, and the gurgling river for company. A couple of days later, we followed the twisting and turning Lewis & Clark Trail along the Lochsa, then the Middle Fork of the Clearwater River.

A night in Lewiston, Idaho, at Hells Gate State Park on the Snake River, then on through Clarkston, Washington, up a long road winding through buckskin hills, to a vast plain with golden fields of wheat stretching to the horizon in every direction. The wind made a ssshhhh-ing sound as it blew over the grain. We spent one hot, sticky night in Richland, Washington, then onward on US-12/I-82 toward Yakima, dreary khaki hills on our left, the Yakima River Valley, green with orchards and vineyards, below us on the right.

Beyond Yakima, we followed US-12, along the Natches, then Tieton Rivers, around a bend, and suddenly the hills were much higher, the spruce and fir trees thicker. Up through those hills to White Pass and lovely Rimrock Lake, where we started seeing snow on peaks. Around one more curve, and there was magnificent Mt. Rainier.

We stayed three nights at Ohanapecosh Campground, Mt. Rainier National Park, tucked in among enormous towering cedars and spruce. The forest is like a sacred place, so big and dense, it swallows up the sound and allows only small slivers of sunlight through. At night, the rushing of the Ohanapecosh River below lulled us to sleep.

Each day we drove to one of the visitor centers for different views of that immense mountain. Alpine wildflowers were blooming everywhere.

From Rainier, we headed to Hoodsport, Washington, on the Olympic Peninsula, then on to Sequim, the self-proclaimed lavender capital of North America. The lavender fields are lovely when the sun breaks through the gray, gloomy weather so typical for this area.

We visited Port Townsend to go on a whale watch trip in the San Juan Islands. Unfortunately, the surrounding scenery was lost in the fog, but occasional pods of orcas came close enough to our boat that we could hear the whoosh of their breathing and get photos of their sleek bodies.

Leaving Sequim, we worked our way down the coast, then inland to Cathlamet, Washington, and a night at a marina on the Columbia River. It was sunny and breezy when we arrived, which made us rejoice, but later it clouded up again. The next stop was Welches, Oregon, to visit some RVing friends who had a camp-host job at Wildwood Recreation Site, on the Salmon River. We spent time with them the next couple of days, hiking in the woods, and driving up to Mt. Hood for a buffet at the Timberline Lodge.

From Welches, we headed back to the coast and Florence, Oregon. At the Sea Lion Caves, we watched the sea lions below us on the rocks. Some were enormous. Those in the surf would catch a surge, heave up onto the rocks, perch on the very edge, weave their heads and necks back and forth for a bit, then plunge in again. They made a constant growling noise. The wind was fierce, and the view magnificent, with the beach curving off into the distance, the breaking waves creating a lacy pattern along the edge.

In Port Orford, Oregon, we overnighted at Cape Blanco State Park. Lovely place, but the beach was windy and fogged in, with temperatures in the mid-50s.

The next day we moved on to Klamath River, California, and stayed at a park right on the river. The Yurok Indians were out with their 100-foot gill nets *destroying the river,* according to a Fish and Game warden we spoke with. The salmon population was down every year as not enough salmon were getting through the nets to spawn. Klamath looked to be a ghost town. It used to be a big logging center with five lumber mills. Now, places are boarded up, the casino is closed, and we heard there were significant drug problems. Sadly, many other villages along the coast had a similar history.

In Redcrest for a night, we were right in the middle of Redwood country. The coastal redwoods are magnificent. They grow to 370 feet or more, and up to 22 inches in diameter. The following day, we left US-101 and continued the journey hugging the coast on CA-1 to Westport-Union Landing State Beach. We parked along the edge of the cliff; the ocean rolled in 70-100 feet below Mehitabel. This wild spot was one of my absolute favorite camping sites.

I pulled out the chairs, made a drink and spent the next few hours reading, and watching Pacific gray whales blowing and feeding out at sea. Two of them dove with flukes up at the same moment. The peaceful view was mesmerizing, and I spent most of the next day out there as well. We explored the tiny town of Westport,  another once-thriving logging town. Vibrant nasturtiums rioted everywhere, climbing over weathered fences and through blackberry bushes, even up into trees.

On September 1, I drove five-plus hours on a twisting two-lane road, the hardest 122 miles I'd ever driven. At one spot, going around a curve, a sheer drop on my right, there was a big crack along the yellow line in the center of the road.

Yikes! I breathed a sigh of relief as I got past it safely, and sometimes wonder if that piece of CA-1 is still there.

There were lots of strange-looking Pepto-Bismol-colored lilies, clusters of them on tall, leafless brownish-red stems, possibly the world's ugliest flower. Also, more nasturtiums which I heard are a pest in this part of the country, re-seeding everywhere. We spent that night in Bodega Bay at Sonoma Coast State Beach, the most dangerous beach in California due to a steep drop-off and a long trough. There were warnings posted everywhere.

The next day, we traveled the last of CA-1, beautiful though hair-raising. Up and down Mt. Tamalpais, over the Golden Gate Bridge, and down 19th Avenue in San Francisco. A parked utility truck, with pipes racked along the side, knocked my side-view mirror catty-wumpus and left it hanging by a wire. After exchanging a startled glance with the driver, I continued to Pacifica, where we stayed five nights at the San Francisco RV Resort. Walking along the edge of the cliff one evening, I saw that there used to be another row for RV parking and guessed it was now somewhere down on the rocks below.

Since Hal was driving his car, I was doing all the RV driving myself, and it was beginning to wear on me. I wanted to be left alone at the end of the day, and Hal wanted my attention. A couple of times, he complained of feeling dizzy, so I was worried about his health as well.

While in Pacifica, we visited each day with Jeff, Laurie, and grandson Jack. Laurie was battling breast cancer and undergoing chemo, but we lucked out on the timing. It was the end of the two-week cycle of treatments, so she was in good shape and seemed to have energy to spare. Being bald gives a person that pared down to the essentials look; it's surprising how distracting hair can be. She looked quite elegant with or without hats and wigs. It was delightful to spend time with them. I was grateful I had not had to go through chemo with my own breast cancer experience but worried about the three of them.

I was having sleep problems and feeling stressed. One night I had my first ever anxiety attack. It felt like I couldn't breathe, and scared me. I got up at 1:30 and took one of Hal's anti-anxiety pills, but it was another hour before I slept. In retrospect, I think my GPS was signaling me that things were not alright, but I didn't make the connection at that time. I hadn't yet learned to tune into my feelings.

Jack came to spend a day with us. He and Hal went fishing off the Pacifica Pier and had a hilarious time to hear them tell it. Jack spent the night with us, and he and I polished off a pound of wild salmon while Hal had a grass-fed steak.

On September 7, we headed inland to the Sacramento Delta and on to Plymouth for a few nights so that I could enjoy a three-day plein air painting workshop nearby.

From Plymouth, we journeyed to Yosemite Lakes RV Park in Groveland, outside Yosemite National Park, where we spent four nights, going into the park each day. I took off by myself one day to sit and sketch in Tuolumne Meadows.

From Yosemite, we traveled to Convict Lake State Park in Inyo National Forest. We got the last available site for one night and would have loved to stay longer as it was a beautiful area. Then to Space Station RV Park in Beatty, Nevada, for two nights so we could have a day to visit Death Valley National Park. That strangely beautiful place is 190' below sea level. The temperature was 113 degrees, and the blacktop in the parking lots was squishy.

After a few nights in Pahrump, Nevada, and a night in Laughlin, Nevada, we crossed the Colorado River into Arizona. We stopped for one night in Wickenburg and, at last, arrived back in Tucson on September 26.

We had traveled almost 6,000 miles since leaving on May 5 and were both ready for a long rest.

———❧❧❧———

All this togetherness was wearing on me. Several times during the past couple of months, I'd gone off for a drive or walk by myself, which bothered Hal.

I was becoming more concerned about certain aspects of this relationship. Hal tended to monopolize conversations when we were with friends and my family. He liked to talk about how he was going to take care of me and buy a house when we got to Tucson. I knew he meant I wouldn't have to worry about money, wouldn't need to work, and would have more time to spend with him. The trouble was I didn't want to be taken care of that way. *Don't Fence Me In* had always been my theme song. He had never understood that about me though I had tried to explain it several times. I was feeling trapped, confined. It was clear I wasn't thriving in this situation, and I needed to figure out what was not working and see what I might change.

My internal GPS had given me occasional warning signs from the beginning, but I'd ignored them, telling myself that every relationship had issues. Now they were getting harder to ignore, and I was beginning to see patterns. Hal had frequently said things to try to separate me from my friends, even my family. "Oh, you should hear what so-and-so says about you," he'd say. I knew he was making it up or twisting their meaning, but why? He hadn't liked me spending so much time with Nancy, saying, "When women get together, they talk about their relationships and things get wrecked."

Where were we headed? An eternal optimist, I told myself if we bought a house and stayed put part of the year, he'd get involved in activities that interested him, there would be more space, and less of this intense togetherness. But would he actually buy something? I had doubts. He often said he was going to do something, but didn't follow through. I could sense a change coming.

··· 18 ···

Decisions

We strengthen our bond with our intuitive nature by listening inwardly at every turn in the road. Should I go this way or this way? Should I stay or go? Should I resist or be flexible? Should I run away or toward? Is this person, event, venture true or false?
— Clarissa Pinkola Estes, *Women Who Run With the Wolves*

BACK IN TUCSON, we spent two months at Far Horizons Tucson Village RV Park. In the center of the park was a big pool and spa where I swam laps several times a week and a terrific fitness center where Hal worked out almost every day. There were rooms with puzzles, a library, a painting room, rooms for stained glass, and sewing, about everything you could need. So we enjoyed our stay there.

Hal had been having health issues since early September, and they were getting worse: chest pains, shortness of breath, and dizziness. He started a round of doctor visits at the VA

Hospital, but we were frustrated with the pace of getting anything done. He had been told by many doctors over the years that his heart rate was way too low, that he needed a pacemaker. We didn't know how long it would take to get one. There was also a problem with his lungs.

Mehitabel was feeling smaller; banging into each other in 280 square feet, plus the stress of the above unknowns, was taking a toll.

We decided to buy a furnished double-wide in a lovely mobile home park. We had seen it a few times and liked it, so we made an offer and received a counter. At that point, Hal sat tight for a couple of weeks. Bijou was still coming up as a problem. He said he would be okay with her, but he'd said that before, so there was that uncomfortable feeling again. I submitted applications to Arizona, Utah, and New Mexico state parks for part-time work-camper jobs next spring and summer that would give me (or us) a site for free. I was starting to make plans for my life whether or not he was a part of it.

I didn't really care about the house. The extra space would be enjoyable if that's what he wanted. Earlier in the relationship, my choice would have been for us to get a bigger RV because I could contribute by selling mine. But at this point, I was glad we had never done that. There was now a little voice in my head telling me: *You need to maintain your independence. Don't sell Mehitabel and end up dependent on Hal.*

Several times he brought up renting a place for a while. I knew we couldn't live full-time in Mehitabel, but I didn't want to move into a rental again. For three years, I'd listened to Hal come up with one plan after another, but he didn't act on them. The health situation didn't help, but I no longer believed that it would be any different if he were 100 percent healthy. He liked talking big, and I was beginning to realize he didn't like my independence.

Bijou came up again a week or so later. "I didn't mind her when we were renting, but I would in my place." With that statement, I'd had it.

I got a call from the ranger at Kodachrome Basin State Park, near Bryce Canyon in Utah. He said I could have a part-time job for three months next summer, in exchange for free hookups for the RV. I'd be working in the visitor center/gift shop, registering campers, and dispensing information. I told him I was not sure if my partner would be with me. The ranger said that wasn't a problem. I picked the second half of the summer and wondered if this work camper plan fell into the same category as the RV/house. When we first discussed it, he said he liked the idea, but he didn't seem to be as interested now.

A couple of weeks before Thanksgiving, we went out to lunch, and Hal informed me he had made a better offer on the double-wide, in his name only, and the seller had accepted. He said he did it because we needed some time apart.

I was stunned. I couldn't believe that Hal would do something that affected my life without even talking it over with me. Yet he'd done this back in South Dakota during our first year RVing, and again when he sold his RV. Why was I so slow to learn?

Sometimes you're ready for a change and, unconsciously, you know it but haven't yet admitted it to yourself. When it comes, not only are you surprised, but it hurts.

I felt wretched and angry, but mostly at myself. I had ignored the warning signs. Hal's ambivalence about Bijou had come up several times over the past three years, yet he seemed to love her, played with her, seemed fine with her, and her problems, so long as it was in MY rig. He couldn't understand why I was upset; according to Hal, I should not get angry about things. I think he needed a Stepford wife.

Our differences were vast, but I had been comfortable with him much of the time and cared a great deal.

At the end of November, he moved into his new home, I left Tucson Village and went to the parking lot at Casino del Sol.

Having no idea how long he meant when he said *time apart*, I decided it didn't matter. I wasn't going to hang around, so I went online to see if I could find a job with a park in the area. I applied for a position at Organ Pipe Cactus National Monument (ORPI), about 125 miles from Tucson, and five miles from the Arizona/Mexico border, right in the heart of drug and gun smuggling territory. They accepted my application.

I drove down to visit the park and met several of the people with whom I'd be working. I also talked with one of the Border Patrol agents who patrol the park. He told me there were always illegals up on the hills, but if we didn't bother them, they wouldn't bother us. I suspected it was safer there than in Tucson, which had the highest crime rate of any city in Arizona.

Soon, I had another job lined up for spring at Petrified Forest National Park in Holbrook, Arizona. The thought of being single again felt good, like being released from confinement. *Embrace the change.*

Part 4

MAKE ADJUSTMENTS & PIVOT (2011-2012)

··· 19 ···

On My Own Again – Organ Pipe

When Sleeping Beauty wakes up, she is almost fifty years old.
— Maxine Kumin

MEHITABEL, BIJOU, AND I moved to Organ Pipe on December 10, and my janitor/maintenance job started the following week. In the VIP (Volunteers in Park) campground, I had full hookups for Mehitabel plus free propane and laundry facilities. A VIP Community building had three freezers and a refrigerator. The Internet didn't work at my site, so I had to take my computer to higher ground and work in my car, which was a bit frustrating.

It felt so good to be doing this. Not that I'd had a secret desire to clean restrooms and mop floors, but it wasn't bad. There were restrooms with showers in the campground and three remote campsites in the park with dumpsters and pit toilets. We worked in pairs to clean the various areas. I would be with my manager Carol, or another of the volunteers, nick-named Shiny. Twice a week, we'd drive out into the desert to check the remote spots. They stayed surprisingly clean.

At least once a week, two or three of us collected trash along the part of the highway that ran through the park, doing a lot of walking out in the sunshine. At the end of my eight-hour workdays, I was wiped out but was getting stronger, and the exercise was great.

Other volunteers worked the kiosk booth, checking people in and collecting fees. I would not have liked being in that booth for several hours a day.

There was no TV unless you had a satellite dish, which I didn't. No radio stations either. I missed listening to NPR and learning what was going on in the world, but not too much. I read a lot, much of it about the park and Arizona history, and enjoyed that.

December was a slow month. The visitor numbers were down from the previous year. There was continual press about drug smuggling, which didn't help. We had several Law Enforcement Rangers (LEs) in the park, young men doing a frequently dangerous job. They watched over us, and the Federal Border Patrol had a significant presence in the area as well.

Hal came down on the 16th and stayed for three nights. We were more relaxed with each other, played poker, and did some hiking. I had been ambivalent about his coming. There was no mention of my sharing the double-wide at some point. On some level, little by little, my thinking was evolving away from that idea.

My work schedule was four days on (Monday through Thursday), then three off. On the day before Christmas, I finished at 1:00 and hurried to take a shower and do laundry as Hal was coming at 3:30. By three, I was up at the Visitor Center, thinking I'd have a half-hour to catch up on email before he arrived. But he got there two minutes after I pulled in.

There was only one grocery store, 35 miles away in Ajo, and the prices were higher than in Tucson. Hal brought things I couldn't find in Ajo. He also brought bags of grapefruit and oranges from the trees at his new place, so he was a welcome visitor in the campground.

I got up early the next morning and made coleslaw and cranberry/orange relish, both of which would go to the camp potluck at noon. I would have loved to take time to relax, read, and be quiet, but Hal kept talking and then played CDs.

We had a hike in Alamo Canyon, then dinner with the other VIPs and Law Enforcement Rangers. The two of us shared a bottle of wine, which may have been a bad idea, then headed back to Mehitabel. I made the mistake of trying to talk about our situation.

He got upset. "Do we have to keep going over and over this?"

Hal thought he had told me a month or two apart, but all he ever said was *some time*, and he never clarified what that meant. He had thought I'd go to one of the RV parks in Tucson and wait.

I told him about my Petrified Forest job; he was not happy about it and asked if anything would make me change my mind.

"Hal, it feels like our relationship is not working anymore, and I don't know if we can put it together again. I like being with you, but I also like being alone. Having you come down right after my workday ends means there is no time for me to regroup, do chores, read, and relax a bit. So that isn't working well for me."

Christmas Day ended in disaster; Hal left for home about five.

I knew Bijou had been part of Hal's decision to buy the mobile home without me, although now he indicated he'd

changed his mind about that. I didn't think I could be comfortable with him in his new home because of the way he had
managed everything. It didn't seem right, after a three-year
relationship, to make a 180-degree change in plans without
talking it over with your partner. He would likely do it again.
I knew I didn't want to be in that sort of relationship. The
bottom line was I didn't trust him. I should have paid a lot
more attention to my inner GPS.

I would probably not have left him alone with his health
problems if he hadn't pretty much sent me off. My parents
raised me to be too responsible, and leaving would have felt
wrong somehow. But Hal had a habit of walking away if he
didn't like the way things were going. If he'd admit that maybe
he went too far too fast and was sorry, I might feel differently,
but he had this sort of righteous attitude about it, as though I
had forced him to make the decision.

The relationship seemed to have run its course; we wanted
different things. I wasn't done with my RV adventures,
though I would concentrate on work-camping jobs now. I
had another job lined up for the second half of summer 2011
at Kodachrome Basin State Park. It felt right to be making
decisions on my own again.

Time alone sounded good to me, and I looked forward
enthusiastically to the coming year. I'd always enjoyed the
time on my own, and I'd longed for it so often during the past
three years. I could feel the stress leaving my body.

There were several black-throated sparrows in the palo
verde next to my rig; they are curious, fat, little birds. Shiny
and I saw a glorious American Kestrel one day on our drive
back from a trash pickup at Pinckley Peak.

The sunrises were spectacular as we headed out at seven
in the mornings to start work. It was a special feeling to be
up greeting the new day as it was born. Both spiritual and
calming to pause and watch the light growing.

Hal didn't make it down for a few weeks though he called several times. He said he missed me, waited a moment for me to say the same, then asked me if I missed him. "I think about you frequently, Hal, but I can't say I miss you." He didn't like that answer.

What did he mean by saying he missed me? Did he long to have me there? Did he want his full-time cook? Two days a week, it might be pleasant to have him around to do things with, but the rest of the time, I enjoyed being alone with Bijou.

I knew by now I was never going to live in his mobile home. I visited it once after he'd moved in. He wanted to show me everything he'd done to it; I started shaking and thought I might get sick. I finally understood that to be in a relationship with Hal meant I would need to give up things that were important to me. I needed quiet time to myself for reading, working on my business, writing. When I was with him, I didn't get that quiet time and felt stressed as a result. Either twenty-odd years of living alone had made me miserable relationship material, or I needed to be with someone who had engrossing interests of his own. It's also possible I was just not capable of being comfortable in someone else's space. I liked having my own home.

So, I was on my own again. It was a relief not to be responsible for another person. I realized that I'd genuinely enjoyed all those years I'd spent alone and had never felt particularly lonely. There's a lot of social pressure to be paired up; on some level, I must have believed I should be. I often disliked the way I felt when I was married or in a steady relationship. Not at first, of course. But the passion dies, at least to some extent, and I felt I'd lost myself, or a part of myself. It kept me from seeing my own needs. I resented losing myself in my marriages, and my relationship with Hal. It was a huge relief when they ended. The feeling of freedom came back, and I could do what I wanted, whenever I wanted.

Was I happy? How do you measure happiness? I watched the sun come up over the Ajo Mountains in the morning, and go down again in the evening, filling the sky with apricot, gold, and magenta. I took the garbage out at night and saw the heavens filled with stars. I watched the feathery clouds curling across the sky during the day, and the black-chinned hummingbird fighting off would-be invaders at his feeder. During all those moments, I had a feeling of peace and contentment. I enjoyed the silence. Would it be better if I shared it with someone? Sometimes, of course, but many times to be alone and witnessing the glory was enough.

I often think that the desert is my home. I'm happy anywhere I can see so much sky. That is my touchstone. I am always aware of it and what it is doing.

—∞∞∞—

February roared in with vicious winds, overnight temperatures in the low 20s, and chilly days. We worked hard to find inside jobs to do.

The freezing temps caused my hose to spring a leak. I cut off about ten feet and fixed it, but a few nights later, there was a second leak at the other end. I repaired that one as well, feeling proud of myself. My water hose was now somewhat shorter, thus easier to coil and store.

Mid-month, I took off early one morning with another volunteer to do the Estes Canyon/Bull Pasture hike. We hiked a total of five miles altogether since we took the wrong path at one point and had to backtrack. There were stunning views, and the weather was terrific. It was a rough uphill climb the second half of the way up, and a steep downhill path back to the parking area. My legs were wobbly on the way down, and I sure slept well that night.

On the 15th, the volunteers went on a field trip to Quitobaquito, an oasis in the National Monument. It had been closed to the public since 2003 due to escalating drug traffic and violence along the border. Two LE rangers stayed nearby to guard us. Others had been posted on top of the surrounding hills two hours before we got there.

Quitobaquito borders the international boundary between the United States and Mexico. Park resource employees work to preserve and protect it as an essential piece of the history of the area: archaeological, cultural, historical, and pre-historically. It had been an important trading center between the Gulf of California and the interior of the U.S. on the Salt Trail, and it was inhabited almost continually for 1,500 years by the various O'odham tribes. By the second half of the 1800s, there were a few colorful non-native residents. Andrew Dorsey came in the 1860s, opened a store, dug irrigation ditches, and deepened the pond. In 1887, Jefferson Davis Milton, a former Texas Ranger, was hired to set up a United States customs and immigration station.

There are natural springs that come out in several places on the slopes of the granite hills to the north. Small canals, now maintained by the park, run from the springs and lead the water to a pond, home to a distinct variety of pupfish on the endangered species list. How did the fish get there? One theory is that they migrated during heavy rains that flooded the area between the pond and the Sonoyta River, about one-quarter mile to the south.

One morning as I went to work, I could smell the rain coming; it's not a scent you often notice in the desert. For the past couple of days, we'd had clouds along with sprinkles of rain, and we all hoped that we'd get enough moisture to make this parched landscape start greening up. As it turned out, we got only two-tenths of an inch from that storm.

After dealing with the leaks at both ends of my hose, I noticed a new hole, right in the middle. I went to Ajo, bought a new hose, attached it a couple of days later, and the next morning it had sprung a leak. I filled my water tank and worked off that for a few days, then went and got another hose and asked maintenance if they could reduce the pressure.

On the 20th, my new water hose sprung a leak! What the heck was going on? The maintenance guys came by to put a pressure reducer on the faucet but told me it wasn't the pressure, and it hadn't been the freeze. It was a pack rat! It looked like he had taken a bite of my electric cable, as well, so I got that up off the ground.

One more new hose. I topped off the water tank, then put the hose away. I was not leaving it around for the pack rat any longer. A few days later, I heard from one of my neighbors in the campground that the evil creature had started in on his hose.

Carol and I headed out to get trash at Alamo Canyon one morning and saw a grand caravan of big, beautiful motorhomes coming toward us, each one representing $100K or more. We thought for a moment that they were going to turn into the park, but they continued, headed for Rocky Point in Mexico. We counted 27, all with green placards in their front windows, so it was a group of some kind.

One of the park employees who lived across the border in Sonoyta took four of us on a journey into the Mexican part of the Sonoran Desert. We traveled through Sonoyta to a small visitor center to access the road leading to the volcanic craters. The land is flatter and less vegetated in Mexico than in the Monument. There were few saguaros, lots of chollas and mesquite, brittlebush, very few rocks on the ground, except close to the hills and mountains. Light-colored sand surrounded us. As we got closer to the craters, the sand got darker, then black.

Our destination was El Elegante, the biggest crater. We were able to drive almost to the top, where we parked and walked up the last bit. It was windy, cold, and overcast. At the edge of the crater, we were almost blown over by the force of the wind. The hole was enormous and deep.

Altogether there are about a dozen Maar craters and more than 400 cinder cones in this biosphere, which is called El Pinacate y Gran Desierto de Altar. It is Organ Pipe's sister park and a fantastic place.

From El Elegante, we retraced our route back to the highway, passing the Sierra Blanca Mountains. We then went to the main visitor center, called Schuk Toak by the Tohono O'odham Indians. Schuk Toak was the first self-sufficient, energy-wise public building in Latin America, with 132 solar panels and a wind generator. It sits on the furthest edge of the lava flow from Pinacate Peak, which erupted some four thousand years ago. Black lava surrounded us, yet every dip and crevice had filled with sand and had ocotillo and brittlebush growing. We saw massive dunes in the distance, the most extensive mobile dunes in North America.

We continued to Rocky Point (Puerto Peñasco) on the edge of the Gulf of California (Sea of Cortez). Rocky Point is a large city, and there's a stark contrast between the new high-rise condos along the beach and the abject poverty seen elsewhere. The high rises were mostly unoccupied, and many were unfinished, probably waiting for a better economy.

We had lunch, wandered to the edge of the sea, and bought some fresh shrimp to take home. Wind-blown sand was everywhere. On the way out of town, we stopped at a supermarket to wander the aisles. There were familiar looking cans and bottles on the shelves, all labeled in Spanish.

The rain started soon after I went to bed that night. The wind, which had blown all day, picked up strength as time went on, rocking Mehitabel and waking me several times. It calmed down and stopped raining in the wee small hours.

We got three-quarters of an inch of rain, and there was snow on the Ajo Mountains in the morning. The desert looked so much lighter and greener, washed clean by that rain. Within a couple of days, many of the ocotillos had tiny green leaves opening, and colors were changing and brightening. The birds were singing their little hearts out in celebration.

Hal came another time or two for brief visits, but there was nothing new. He was through RVing; I wasn't. I had no regrets.

··· 20 ···

Happenings

Wisdom comes with the ability to be still. Just look and just listen. No more is needed. Being still, looking, and listening activates the non-conceptual intelligence within you. Let stillness direct your words and actions. — Eckhart Tolle

MARCH 2011 HAD us watching the government limp along two weeks at a time, on the verge of a shutdown. We were curious as to what would happen if everything came to a screeching halt, and ORPI had to shut down. It might have been interesting, but it didn't happen.

My last week at Organ Pipe, desert lupine and globemallow started to bloom along the roads. Bright yellow flowers covered the brittlebush, and many of the ocotillos dressed up in vivid green leaves about the size of my little fingernail, transforming the dead-looking, spiny stalks. Some ocotillo and palo verde had leaves, and others remained bare. You could barely see the tiny leaves on the palo verde, but they gave the tree a fuller appearance. The bright mahogany-red Mexican jumping bean leaves were turning green. Jojoba leaves started changing from gray-green to gold.

During that last week, I banged one of my rear tires on a big rock in front of the VIP building. I looked and, as it seemed fine, drove on to the administration building to pick up my mail. While I chatted with folks in there, the tire went completely flat.

I had to empty my entire trunk to get at the donut spare tire. The Superintendent and his right-hand man came out and removed the flat. They said there was no chance of sealing and pumping it up, so they put on the spare for me.

There was not a single 15-inch tire, new or used, in Ajo. I planned to tow the car, with the donut, back to Tucson on Friday morning, unhitch it and go to Walmart to get a new tire put on.

The terrific guys in maintenance had other thoughts about my plan. They claimed it wasn't safe towing the car with the donut. Sue, at the Visitor Center, worried about that, too. She was driving up to Phoenix for a workshop and could stop and pick up a tire for me. Kenny, in maintenance, said he would mount it on the rim first thing Friday morning. So, I got on the phone to a tire dealer and set things up.

Friday morning, a new tire was all mounted and ready for me. I took off the donut, put on the new tire, and hit the road a little after nine.

When I got within 30 miles of Tucson, I turned on the radio and tuned in NPR. That was when I heard about the massive earthquake in Northern Japan. After three months with no radio or TV, it was so strange to discover that, oh yeah, there was another world out there and things were happening in it.

A little after noon, I arrived at Casino del Sol, which would be my home for the next couple of weeks. There were

25-30 rigs all boondocking there, but after the first week, many of them left.

Over the next few days, I bought a new spare tire (a real one), balanced my other new tire, and got rid of the donut. I immersed myself in all the things I had missed, wandering through Walmart and Whole Foods, and listening to NPR.

I took Mehitabel to dump the holding tanks and fill with water on the 17th and creamed the back left bumper on a concrete post next to the sewer drain. Trouble usually comes in threes; what would the next surprise be?

I turned 69. My brother Chris called to wish me a happy birthday. What with everything else going on, I had forgotten it was my birthday, but he remembered, which had not happened for the past ten years or so.

The weather was cooling off a bit; it was comfortable boondocking at the Casino, and quiet at night. A big hotel was under construction, and trucks arrived early in the morning, but that was no problem, as I had developed a habit of waking well before sunrise.

During my two-week stay at Casino del Sol, I sat with my coffee early one morning, gazing at the big Allegro motorhome parked in front of me. The couple who lived in it looked to be in their late 70s. I had seen them going to and from the Casino a couple of times. Their rig was facing mine, and their front curtains were not completely closed. I thought they were dancing, but as I continued to watch, it became clear they were exercising. They kept it up for a good half hour, bouncing up and down, jumping one way then the other, flinging their arms over their heads and down again. They looked as though they were having an excellent time.

On March 27, I moved up to Catalina State Park for two nights. It's a beautiful park north of the city, with large RV sites, electric and water hookups, spotless restrooms, and showers. It sits at the foot of Pusch Ridge, a line of jagged mountains, razorback ridges, and deep canyons. Gnarled mesquite trees, still without leaves, were everywhere in the park. Saguaros were scattered on the nearby hills.

On the 29th, I drove north to Phoenix, then to Cliff Castle Casino in Camp Verde for two nights. On the 31st, I continued north toward Flagstaff and the snow-covered San Francisco Peaks, then took I-40 East to Petrified Forest National Park (PEFO), my next job.

••• 21 •••

Petrified Forest

Anyone who stops learning is old, whether at twenty or eighty.
Anyone who keeps learning stays young.
— Henry Ford, American Industrialist

BELIEVE IT OR not, my new tire went flat as a pancake (the third thing), and I had to buy another. It turned out there was a cut/split on the inside edge under the rim, so it was leaking air, and there was no way to fix it. That made three new tires in a month, plus the bodywork on the RVs rear bumper. I hoped that would be the end of my tire saga.

I'd seen the following birds at PEFO already: Say's Phoebe, white-crowned sparrows, chipping sparrows, killdeer, ravens, goldfinches, brown-headed cowbirds, American crows, and a Northern Harrier. I'd also seen several pronghorns, a family of cottontails, and a couple of black-tailed jackrabbits.

When I first arrived, the rangers presented me with a backpack containing approximately 30 pounds of books (on loan only). I'd worked my way through about ten pounds. Reading and listening to the Rangers do their programs constitutes training in the off-season. The learning curve for this job was quite a bit higher than that required for cleaning bathrooms and collecting trash. I was busy absorbing as much as possible, so I could start presenting interpretive programs.

My debut as an Interpretive Ranger finally took place. I started at Puerco Pueblo, a partially excavated archeological site occupied about 700 years ago. Next was the Painted Desert Inn. The Inn's history covers the Civilian Conservation Corps, Fred Harvey Co., and the Harvey Girls, murals by Fred Kabotie, a well-known Hopi artist, and the interior design redo by Mary Colter. Visitors were generally quite interested in learning about the park, so there were lots of questions. After a couple of weeks, I added the Triassic period to my routine, covering the presumed events of 220 million years ago that resulted in the beautiful petrified wood, and the wicked-looking reptiles, amphibians, and little dinosaurs that roamed the area in those days.

The wind was ferocious at times. Late afternoon programs at Puerco had me gasping for air and chewing dust.

Add yellow-headed blackbirds to my bird list. They showed up and hung out in one of the big trees near our RV sites. Stunning birds, with beautiful bright gold heads and breasts, all else black except for one white bar on the underside of the wings.

On the afternoon of April 27, *I was standin' on the corner in Winslow, Arizona.* That was exciting as it had been a month since I'd been any farther than the Safeway in Holbrook.

After visiting the Chamber of Commerce, located in the old Hubbell Trading Post building on 2nd Avenue, I had an elegant lunch at La Posada. This incredible inn was the last great railroad hotel built by the Fred Harvey Co. It is bounded on the south side by the Santa Fe/Burlington Northern Railroad, on the north by Historic Route 66, the Mother Road. Architect/designer Mary Colter sure knew what she was doing; it's gorgeous.

After wandering through the Old Trails Museum, I drove up to Homolovi State Park and hiked around the large excavated pueblo dwelling. There were holes everywhere, as the ruins had been thoroughly dug over by pot hunters before park status protected them.

One morning I went with Ranger Steve and a large group of geology students from Canada for a hike to The Dying Grounds, where there are beautiful shards of petrified wood and fossils everywhere.

We had a photographer as the artist-in-residence for a few weeks. She and I went out one evening to take photos at Kachina Point, then drove halfway down the park, arriving just in time to catch the last light on the Teepees.

The lizards were out in force, which likely meant snakes were out as well though I saw none. I saw two common side-blotched lizards and a whiptail lizard that ran like hell every time I tried to get close. It finally stopped for a bit, its sides heaving like little bellows. The beautiful collared lizards in the park seemed quite happy to pose for photos.

Early one morning, I hiked the steep trail at Kachina Point down into the badlands, then out past the big dunes. Hiking back up had me gasping for breath. It takes at least three months to get adjusted to the altitude; it has something to do with your red blood cells getting larger.

Part of my job was roving the trails and answering questions. I also had to warn visitors to stay on the trails and not to pocket any of the petrified wood, a responsibility I took quite seriously.

Wildflowers bloomed throughout the park, and heavy seed heads developed on the various grasses. The wind seldom stopped except late at night. They told me it would end on June 1, and we would all wish for it to come back.

June first had come and gone, but the wind was still blowing. We were thankful for that as it was getting hot and smoke from the vast Wallow fire to the southeast lay over the park at night and in the early morning. It took the wind, which started mid-morning, to clear it out.

I'd been doing a lot of reading and two biographies, in particular, fascinated me. One was about Annie Montague Alexander (1869-1950), who collected fossils, then mammals, birds, and plants. She started and endowed both the Museum of Vertebrate Zoology and the Museum of Paleontology at the University of California at Berkeley. At one point, she spent time collecting at Petrified Forest. She never married, but had a companion, Louise Kellogg, for the last 40 years of her life. I learned that relationship was called a Boston Marriage.

The other book was about Mary Colter, who lived during that same period and worked for both the Harvey Co. and the Santa Fe Railroad. She designed and decorated several of the Harvey hotels along the railroad in New Mexico and Arizona and is noted for the buildings she developed at Grand Canyon National Park: Hermit House, Watchtower, and Phantom Ranch.

These brave and strong women did their own thing, irrespective of what society expected of them at the time, and they achieved so much. I truly admired them. They reminded me of my Aunt Nita and Hickey, those courageous and adventurous women in my past.

Most work-days. I walked five miles or so on the trails and in the visitor centers. One early morning, I saw two fox kits, or coyote pups, down near the Crystal Forest Trail. They were so cute, and one of them was a curious fellow. He sat and watched me as I came close. Mom was nowhere in evidence, out hunting for breakfast, no doubt.

It was breeding season for the collared lizards; I'd seen two or three females, usually with a male nearby. The females were shy and hurried into hiding the minute I approached, so it was difficult to get a photo of them.

A pair of Western Tanagers showed up. They are beautiful birds and are usually forest dwellers. I assumed they were on their way to the White Mountains, but then saw them again. The smoke was perhaps too thick in the mountains, which are near where the fire was blazing away.

Once school was out, we saw lots of kids in the park. The Jr. Ranger Program in the national parks is popular with families. The kids are given a book and must complete several activities and answer a couple of questions. Then a ranger swears them in and gives them a badge and a patch. They are so proud, as are their parents. One day there were two young boys, both with blue-jean jackets. Pins from various parks covered the fronts, and their mother had sewn all the patches onto the backs.

One day I watched a pair of house finches courting. There was no doubt about what the male was doing. He sang, flipping his tail up and down, doing little twirls in front of his lady. It appeared she was ignoring him though she didn't fly away. She was just playing it cool.

··· 22 ···

Moving On To
Kodachrome Basin

*There are only two ways to live your life. One is as though
nothing is a miracle. The other is as though everything is a
miracle.* — Albert Einstein

THE WALLOW FIRE continued to burn through June. It was
finally 100 percent contained, though it burned well over
800 square miles and was tagged the most significant fire in
Arizona history.

We saw smoke toward the southwest one afternoon and
later learned that a trailer (as in RV) blew a tire which ignited
the grass. It got controlled quickly, which was lucky, as the
wind would have brought that one straight to us.

One morning I hiked the Lacey Point trail with some of
the other volunteers and Ranger Steve. We started at 8:30
and got back about noon, so the return trip was hot and

sweaty. It was beautiful out in the badlands; we saw marvelous petroglyphs at Jitterbug Rock, beautiful pieces of petrified wood, and lots of pottery shards at an ancient archaeological site. It was steep climbing back up onto the mesa; by the time I reached the top, the heat and the wind had worn me out.

A killdeer made its nest on the ground under a tree in the VIP area. There were three gray-speckled eggs that the

male and female took turns guarding. As we couldn't tell them apart, we nicknamed them both Doug. If we walked too close to the nest, Doug would run, acting as though he were wounded to lure us away. We were all anxiously waiting for the chicks to hatch. The parents do not feed them in the nest. The minute they hatch, they are off and running, so you must be watching at the right moment. Unfortunately, the great hatch didn't occur before I left PEFO.

By the July 4th weekend, we were in the transition period between the hot, dry weather and the monsoon season. The humidity increased to about 30 percent; every afternoon, clouds built, and we could see lightning in the distance. Aside from a couple of brief showers, most of the rain did not make it into the north end of the park. Temperatures were in the upper 90s. The wind left us at last, and, yes, I wished it were back.

———◁∕∘∕∘▷———

On July 8, I left Petrified Forest and headed to Flagstaff, driving through a violent rainstorm before arriving at Greer's Pine

Country RV Park, where I spent the next four nights. It was cool there—a good ten or so degrees cooler than PEFO—what bliss. I hooked up Mehitabel, then went to Albertson's and New Frontiers Natural Marketplace. Imagine my joy when I discovered arugula and crisp, fresh, dewy baby bok choy, as well as some delicious-looking veggie pizza in the deli. I had missed good vegetables so much.

While in Flagstaff, I visited Walnut Canyon National Monument. I hiked the Island Trail, which led me partway down into the canyon past thousand-year-old cliff dwellings once occupied by the Sinagua people (Sinagua is Spanish for *people without water*). They farmed the cliff rims, building their homes about one-third of the way down in shallow caves, which had eroded out of the limestone cliffs. Archaeologists believe it was the women who were the builders. Hmmm.

On a rainy morning, I visited the Museum of Northern Arizona, devoted to the geology and anthropology of the Colorado Plateau. Pottery and basketry from all the different periods of occupation and all the different tribes were displayed. The gift shop featured beautiful arts and crafts of the present-day Hopi, Zuni, and Navajo.

That afternoon I drove out to Sunset Crater Volcano and Wupatki National Monuments. Sunset Crater erupted between 1040 and 1100, the most recent in a six-million-year history of volcanic activity around Flagstaff. The immediate area surrounding the crater consists of vast lava beds and hills of cinders, a stark and beautiful landscape. Even miles away, cinders covered the earth. The plant life was brilliant against the black.

Wupatki is a collection of several masonry pueblos or villages. It was home to thousands of people by 1180, farming where the thin layer of ash from the eruption of Sunset Crater helped hold the moisture. By 1250, the people had moved on to establish new homes, and the pueblos were empty.

On July 13, I drove up to Page and Lake Powell/Glen Canyon National Recreation Area. The scenery was incredible: canyons, cliffs, and domes of red rock. I stopped to get gas at the Shell station. As I stood there, hose in hand, the heavens let loose, and I got drenched. I toweled off and continued the few miles over the Glen Canyon Dam and on to Wahweap Bay for two nights at the Lower Wahweap RV Campground.

The next day I boarded a cruise boat with many others and enjoyed a cruise out to Rainbow Bridge National Monument. It was a gorgeous sunny day. There were puffy clouds and a gentle breeze, no sign of rain, vistas of red sandstone rocks and  cliffs against the blue-green of the water. The bridge itself is a marvel of nature, 290 feet high and 250 feet wide. It's on Navajo land and considered sacred by them. Here's an old photo of my Aunt Nita on horseback at Rainbow Bridge; it probably dates from the 1930s or 40s, well before the dam created the lake.

On the 14th, I drove 183 miles to Kodachrome Basin State Park in the middle of Grand Staircase-Escalante National Monument in Utah. Incredibly, the cliffs got even redder, especially after turning onto SR12 and entering Dixie National Forest and the Red Canyon. I drove past the entrance to Bryce Canyon, and through the little towns of Tropic and Cannonville. The cliffs and hoodoos along the way showed an incredible array of colors: tan, ochre, pink, coral, terra cotta, and red. Finally, I arrived at my destination.

At Kodachrome, Mehitabel sat all alone, with full hookups, next to the visitor center parking lot. At the end of July, when the current camp host would leave his site in the campground, I expected to move up there. There was no cell service in the park; I had to drive nine miles to Cannonville to get a signal. No internet service either, but there was a DSL line in the Visitor Center, which I was welcome to use.

The recent rainstorms had resulted in leaks around the skylight over my shower. I got up on the roof and did a pretty messy caulking job.

I soon discovered that I wouldn't be a camp host in the campground. A couple would arrive at the end of the month to fill that position. I'd heard that camp host jobs go to couples rather than singles, which is too bad. The plan was for me to work just at the Visitor Center. My parking space felt pretty isolated, especially after nine at night, when the doors closed. I kept the curtains closed all the time, partly to block the sun, but also because everyone driving through the parking area looked into my rig. There was a signpost, covered with a plastic bag, at the front of the space. After a week or so,

the bag was removed— the sign read, *Camp Host*.

After that, every few nights, a late arrival knocked on my door around ten. "I have a reservation and don't know where to go." I'd been ready to turn out the light, but would throw on a robe and give them directions through the window. I talked to Aaron, the park supervisor. With no cell service, I had no way to contact anyone should there be a problem. I'm relatively brave but felt vulnerable in this spot.

Aaron told me I could move my rig into the ranger housing area—there was a site with hookups—so on August 10, I moved Mehitabel to the new spot. The bag went back over the camp host sign.

Now red cliffs and sedimentary pipes surrounded me, and I could leave my curtains open. The ranger houses were nearby. Liz and Rachel, the two ranger aides, lived in one, Aaron and his wife in another. There was an ancient juniper which gave late afternoon shade over the picnic table. I was delighted with my new location.

Every morning and late afternoon, a cowboy led a string of saddled horses along the road right behind my rig. There was a riding concession in the park, and the horses overnighted in a corral nearby. I hoped to go on one of the rides in mid-September once the heat abated.

··· 23 ···

Full-Time Ranger Aide

There is only one danger I find in life, you may take too many precautions. — Alfred Adler, Psychologist

AARON OVERHEARD ME talking to Liz one morning about my need in the future to work full-time part of the year to make some money. He said he was looking for another employee and asked if I wanted the job. I jumped at the chance, spent an hour or so filling out reams of paperwork, and waited for it all to go through the system. A week later, I became official, a ranger aide until the end of October.

Another tire went flat on my car. Good grief! I put on the spare and took the flat up to a service place at Bryce Canyon for repairs.

I had worn a dress just once in my four years of RVing, so I filled a 13-gallon garbage bag with almost all the useless *dress* clothes I brought with me. I took it, along with two pairs of shoes, up to the Post Office/Library/Health Clinic in Cannonville, which seemed to have a separate life as a Goodwill location. It felt good to get rid of all that stuff.

On a free day at the end of July, I drove to Cedar Breaks National Monument, almost two hours away. The elevation is a bit over 10,000 feet, and the wildflowers were gorgeous: lupine, larkspur, Markagunt Penstemon, white and pale blue columbine, Indian paintbrush, and sunflowers galore. I saw three dead deer on the road, one live doe, two herds of sheep (brought up to graze during the summer), and two big woodchucks.

The hiking was lovely in the park, and there were plenty more hikes in the 1.9 million-acre Grand Staircase-Escalante Monument. I got out and walked in the early mornings occasionally and after seven in the evenings, longing for cooler weather to explore further.

The heat and humidity finally started to dissipate. We watched big dark clouds massing to the south and west, but most of them bypassed us, drenching Bryce Canyon and Escalante. Finally, there were a couple of downpours that sent red mud filling the gullies and flooding over the roads in the campground.

My caulking job around the skylight over the shower had stayed dry during some light rainstorms, but the hard rain found a way to get in. So, up onto the roof with the caulking gun again. I had my fingers crossed.

Kodachrome Basin was home to many hummingbirds that love the Indian Paintbrush. I walked one evening, and two pairs were swooping and diving close to my head, the hum of their wings quite loud as they buzzed by, making their tiny high-pitched squeaks. Most of them were black-throated hummingbirds.

One day, a hummingbird flew into the office, bounced off the blinds, and fell onto the counter. She was okay and started flying again, trying to find a way out. Rachel and I did our best to guide her toward the door, but it didn't work. She would bang into something and fall, rest a moment, then try again. Finally, I cupped my hands around her and walked to the door. I opened my hands as we got out, and off she flew up into the juniper, a happy hummer again.

She was back again the next day. We found her in the gift shop floor, and Aaron tried to get her to eat at the feeder. She was too weak, however, and just sat on his desk, trying to recover. She didn't.

Before going back to the office after lunch one day, I put up my big awning, thinking to block the late afternoon sun. The wind was light for the most part, but there must have been at least one gust that hit it right, as it was ripped half off and hanging when I returned. I rolled it up again; one more thing to take care of when I got back to Tucson in November.

It was good that I was working full time and getting paid, as I had to buy a new laptop. Mine was six years old and had started to do squirrelly things. I figured I better bite the bullet before I lost everything—what a horrid thought. The prospect of losing all the information on the computer is the stuff of nightmares.

One afternoon I drove up to Escalante and halfway to Boulder. The drive was incredible, climbing up to 7,600 feet with a grand view of Powell Peak, the highest member of the Grand Staircase. The BLM visitor center in Escalante was full of information; they would be hosting an art show that coming weekend that I looked forward to seeing.

I hiked the Mossy Cave Trail on the way up to Bryce Canyon one morning. The cave was unexciting, but the *Big Ditch*, an irrigation ditch that had been dug through the canyon to provide water to the town of Tropic, was neat. Several hikers were wading in the water, and there was a lovely little waterfall.

—∽∽∽—

My dad's heart was wearing out. They had moved him into the long-term-care unit at the assisted-living facility where he lived in Westborough, Massachusetts. I made plans for a quick trip East to visit him. Rachel said she would feed Bijou while I was away.

I drove the five-hour-trip to Salt Lake City after work, stayed at a motel overnight, and took a taxi to the airport the next morning. My son Brian picked me up at the Manchester, New Hampshire, airport, and we went out for a sushi dinner.

The next day, we went to see Dad, wheeled him out into a glorious day, and spent time visiting. He was still my sweet dad, but there was less of him available. He seemed to be occupying some other dimension and said life was dreamlike, like a fantasy. It was so good to see him. Steve and Jon, two of my brothers, were there as well, and I got to spend time with Brian and two of my grandchildren that evening at dinner. Early the next morning, I flew back to Salt Lake City, one day ahead of Hurricane Irene.

••• 24 •••

Exploring The Grand Staircase

The finest workers of stone are not copper or steel tools, but the gentle touches of air and water working at their leisure with a liberal allowance of time.
— Henry David Thoreau

WHAT THOREAU MAY not have known is that air and water are not always gentle in these parts. Not only do they create incredibly strange shapes, but they also generate mud and flash floods throughout the Grand Staircase. Devil's Garden is 14 miles down Hole in the Rock Road past the town of Escalante—well worth the trip to see those incredible shapes. I was warned not to drive any further on that road.

In October, I explored Grand Staircase-Escalante National Monument, traveling a few of the unimproved roads that wandered through the nearly two-million acres.

I braved Cottonwood Canyon Road and drove the eleven miles (40 minutes each way) out to Grosvenor Arch, the second-largest arch, actually a double arch, in Utah. Rainbow Bridge, which I visited on the way up here, is thought to be the largest natural bridge in the world. There are over three-thousand natural arches and bridges scattered throughout Utah. Wind and rain create the arches; flowing water carves the bridges.

Twice, I left Kodachrome State Park and the Grand Staircase, making the trip to a Walmart, two hours away in Cedar City, winding up and down on UT-14 through Cedar Canyon the first time. The most important item on my list, a new water filter with flexible hose extension, was out of stock. But I discovered one of my windshield wipers was falling apart, practiced being a helpless female, and asked a gentleman parked next to me if he knew how to take it off. He kindly did that, and I took it in to get a replacement. Unable to figure out how to put the new blade on, feeling inept, I asked another gentleman if he knew how to install it. He did. Gosh, I was getting good at this. I should have started asking for help sooner in my life.

My second trip was two days after a big rainstorm in the park. Everything above 6,900 feet had gotten a dusting of snow. There had been a storm-caused rockslide on the Cedar Canyon road, so I took UT-20 across to I-15. The mountains to my north were completely white.

The Escalante Canyon Arts Festival is also known as Everett Reuss Days. Reuss was a young man with an endless fascination for this area. He wandered all over it, alone and penniless most of the time, painting and writing. He disappeared into the Escalante River region in 1934, a few months shy of his 21st birthday. I had read a National Geographic story about finding his body in 2009, but at the festival, I learned that story was considered incorrect. Forensic evidence had shown it was a white male of the appropriate age, but DNA samples from Everett's niece and nephew did not provide a good enough match. Now there was a new book *Finding Everett Reuss*. So the mystery continues.

Trees were turning—I saw lovely splashes of yellow, burgundy, rose, and orange at the higher elevations in the Grand Staircase. In the park, the four-wing saltbush turned pale gold, the big sagebrush was blooming, and Indian Paintbrush sported pretty green seedpods.

One of our German visitors drove the 1.5-mile gravel road out to Chimney Rock on a rainy afternoon, and his battery died. He got a lift back to the Visitor Center and came in looking for help. I had jumper cables, so I drove him back to his car. Neither one of us had ever done this before, but after reading the directions, we hooked the cables up and got his car started. He was grateful, and I was plenty pleased with myself and very muddy.

One morning, I headed for Capitol Reef National Park, a 2.5-hour drive that took me almost four hours. I'd heard good things about Escalante Outfitters, so I stopped in to visit. It turned out to be an outdoor gear store/liquor store/bookstore/restaurant, an unusual combination. On the road again, I stopped several times to take photos and had a delicious lunch at Kiva Coffee House, which is set into and on a cliff overlooking the Escalante River Canyon.

The aspens were bright yellow-green with touches of orange and sparkled in the sun at the lower elevations. There's a 9,600-foot ridge between Boulder and Torrey; piles of snow were still around from the storm the week before. I drove up and up, stopping at the overlooks with beautiful views of Capitol Reef and the Henry Mountains. Then I started down again, through the town of Torrey, to Highway 24, which parallels the Reef.

I visited the Visitor Center in the historic village of Fruita. Though it never consisted of more than about 300 acres, Fruita became significant due to the long growing season and abundant water from the Fremont River. Settlers from nearby Torrey and Loa came to the area and planted thousands of fruit trees: many varieties of apples, apricots, peaches, pears, and plums. There are also ancient Fremont cottonwoods with massive twisted trunks. The U.S. government started buying up land in the 1950s. Today the town is a semi-preserved, well-managed historic district containing cabins, a one-room schoolhouse, barns, and the orchards. The National Park Service runs it all.

Capitol Reef, on the eastern edge of Grand Staircase-Escalante, is 100 miles long. It's defined by the Waterpocket Fold, a classic monocline, or fold, with one steep side, in an area of horizontal layers. Between 50-70 million years ago, the sub-surface rocks lifted about 7,000 feet. The overlying layers of rock draped over the fault, creating the Waterpocket Fold. It is quite spectacular. The colors range from yellow to orange to reddish-brown and purple, even light blue, dark green, and bright white. Iron is the most prevalent coloring agent. My drive took me along the cliff on the West side of the Fold; I had hoped to go back on the Notom Bullfrog Road, another unimproved road, but the rangers at the Visitor Center advised against it because of the recent heavy snow.

Fremont Indians occupied this area starting in the 700s. I drove about a mile past the Visitor Center on Highway 24 to see the outstanding Fremont petroglyphs, then started back. The late afternoon light on the many cliffs was beautiful, so I had to stop several times for photos. Way too much driving, but Capitol Reef was worth it.

I'd be leaving this beautiful canyon country soon and was disappointed that I hadn't had time to do much hiking. I didn't hike Bryce Canyon or the trails at Red Canyon, and I never rode the horse out to Cool Cave in the park. Oh well, I could come back some other day.

··· 25 ···

Back In Tucson. You Again?

We either make ourselves miserable or we make ourselves strong. The amount of work is the same.
— Carlos Castenada

I LEFT KODACHROME Basin on October 25, 2011, headed to Tucson. The first night on the road was spent at Walmart in Page, Arizona. It rained hard that night—why did it rain every time I went through Page? However, my third attempt at caulking the skylight seemed to have done the trick, as there were no leaks.

Arriving in Tucson on October 28, I headed for Casino del Sol and discovered the furthest parking lot jammed with RVs. What was going on? Someone came over to my window as I sat there in shock and asked if I was there for the Desert Bluegrass Festival. Well, I guessed I was—how delightful.

There was a message from my brother Steve in Massachusetts, so I called him back and discovered that Dad had gone into the hospital, and they didn't expect him to make it through the day. Later that evening, Steve called to tell me Dad had seemed stable, so he'd left to get dinner, and Dad died twenty minutes after he left. His favorite nurse was with him stroking his back, and Dad just slipped away. He had turned 95 a few weeks before, so he lived a good long life. I was so thankful that I had made the trip to see him at the end of August. I'd heard from several people that it's quite common for patients at the end of life to wait until family members leave before they relax and let go. It's sad to lose a parent, but there's a sense of inevitability to it. I was grateful he had stayed quite healthy throughout his life. He was a marvelous Dad; I was always so proud of him.

That evening there was a free concert. There were six bands in competition, so I went over to listen for a bit. As I worked in my rig the next couple of days, I heard the plinking of banjos and mandolins, the deep beat of a bass, and the strumming of guitars as groups of passionate bluegrass fans got together and jammed.

When the casino had big concerts, all motorhomes had to move out. The grand opening of the new hotel, as well as a Tim McGraw concert, would be the next weekend, so I took Mehitabel over to the Gilbert Ray Campground in Tucson Mountain Park for three nights. There, surrounded by cactus, mesquite, and palo verde, I woke each morning to a chorus of coyotes yipping as they greeted the sun.

I had appointments lined up with doctors, dentists, and vets. I saw my oncologist for the annual checkup. I was worried about a bump that had been growing over the past few months, next to the site of the lumpectomy done seven years ago. He said it needed to be checked and scheduled an appointment with a surgeon.

Over the next two weeks, life took an unexpected and upsetting turn. The surgeon did not like what she saw.

"Since you had radiation the last time, if this proves to be cancer, your only option will be a mastectomy." That was a shock.

I wasn't too surprised when the biopsy confirmed it was cancer. I'd been braless for years; removing just one breast would mean I'd have to wear a bra to contain a prosthetic. Either that or undergo additional surgery for reconstruction. I'd also be holding my breath, wondering if cancer would show up in the other breast. I talked with friends, did some research, and discovered there was a tribe of breastless women out there. I'd never had large breasts; though not loving the idea of losing them, they weren't a significant part of my identity. More important, in my mind, was my determination to put breast cancer behind me for good.

By the time I saw the surgeon again, I'd made my decision and told her I would have a bilateral mastectomy with no reconstruction. Surgery got scheduled for the twelfth of December. The oncologist would determine if I needed chemo. My next appointment with him was the end of November.

I assumed that recovery would be difficult if I stayed in the RV. So, between these appointments, I looked for and found an apartment, got new glasses, bought a bed, then visited a couple of used furniture stores to scrounge for the incidentals I'd need. I also took Mehitabel in for servicing twice, which ate up a whole day each time. So, I concentrated on the things that weren't scary and kept moving forward.

I felt overwhelmed and was so grateful for the support and encouragement I received from family and friends, as well as from people I didn't even know. As a member of the Escapees RV Club, I had earlier contacted another Tucson member, Gail, to see if we could get together while I was in town. We had talked once. She happened to call again the day I got the bad news. When I told her, the first words out of her mouth were, "What can I do to help?" She offered to take me, and Bijou, to stay at her house for a couple of days after the surgery. Another woman, alerted by a mutual friend, invited me for Thanksgiving.

While I certainly wasn't thrilled at having cancer again and was nervous about the surgery, it would do me no good to sit and whine. I would be all right. I looked forward to spending the winter in Tucson, making friends, and taking drawing and painting workshops. Much as I loved RVing, it would be nice to be off the road for a while.

I spent Thanksgiving with two of these new friends, Sharon and George. I took Mehitabel up to Catalina State Park for the night as it was near their home. The next day I went back to Casino del Sol.

On November 27, as I worked on my computer, I became aware of constant rumbling and finally took a break to look out the window.

Renegade Classics, a local biker outlet, and the Salvation Army were sponsoring a Run for Toys. The parking lot had filled with approximately 1000 motorcycles, many of them decorated for Christmas. Every biker had brought something, so there were toys galore—all for underprivileged children in Tucson. It was a fantastic sight.

When I saw the oncologist on November 29, he told me I would not have to have chemo. He called my cancer a *favorable tumor*, a strange combination of words to my mind. I took that to mean it would not tend to run rampant throughout my body.

I woke up in the wee small hours most nights, and my mind started racing about things to move, where to put them, putting the RV in storage, the upcoming surgery. I'd be awake for a couple of hours until I could turn on NPR at five. Other voices helped me let go of my own, and I could doze off again.

On the weekend of December 3 and 4, I moved out of the RV and into the apartment. Sharon and George came over with a futon sofa they were loaning me; we crawled around on the floor for quite a while before we figured out how to put it together.

On Monday, I went back to Mehitabel and took her to the dump station to empty all the tanks. Back at the storage place, I poured antifreeze down the toilet and sink, covered the tires, and left her, which was more than a little heartbreaking. The plan was that on Sunday, December 11, Bijou, and I would go to Gail's house for the next few days. But Bijou had other ideas. With yowls of anger and a fair amount of my blood spilled, she made it clear she was not going anywhere. So be it. We spent Sunday night at the apartment, and on Monday morning, Gail picked me up and took me to the hospital. We left Bijou behind.

One night in the hospital, two nights with Gail, then back to the apartment to find that Bijou had survived my absence with no ill effects. I went out each day for brief errands. I took frequent naps that first week and started to feel somewhat normal again. I had anticipated more difficulty with the recovery phase, so I was surprised at how well things were going.

After my mastectomy, while I was getting used to my new shape, I became hyper-aware of women's breasts. Every woman walking toward me seemed to have enormous breasts; how was it possible they could walk upright?

The first art workshop I signed up for would start on January 21. It felt strange not to have a job taking up a good part of the week, so I was looking forward to getting involved in art, and maybe a hiking club.

On the next visit to the oncologist, he said I should have the *Oncotype* test before determining that chemo would not be necessary. The test was fairly new, but I wondered why he hadn't thought of that a month ago before telling me I would not need chemo. Okay, more waiting, but I'd stay busy discovering Tucson.

The oncologist had started me on the aromatase inhibitor after my surgery. I'd never liked taking pills and knew that doctors tend to prescribe them at the drop of a hat. For some reason, starting on them was one of the scariest and most anxious times I had through the whole experience. It felt as though I were starting down a slippery slope, and the end could not be good. I would have to stop taking them if I started chemo, but once finished, I'd be on them for five years. I was having a lot of trouble sleeping, one of the side effects, and not a good thing. He gave me a prescription for a sleeping pill. I didn't stay on them long, starting a meditation practice instead, which helped.

I've ended up believing none of the doctors know much. They gamble on a set of chemicals because it has seemed to work in the past. It was all up to me. I'd done what they recommended and was taking the estrogen blocker this time, but it may be more about diet, exercise, and lifestyle, about which the doctors know little or nothing. This time, I took my daughter-in-law's advice and joined a support group. Wonderful women, all of them going through various stages of breast cancer. Being a part of the group helped.

As usual, I did lots of reading when I wasn't wandering Tucson: books about cancer and spirituality, as well as escape novels.

I walked several times a week along the Rillito River wash (no water), which was near the apartment, and was trying to loosen up my body and do yoga again. Gail and I went hiking in Sabino Canyon one day; there was water there.

Everything was proceeding smoothly, then on February 3, my oncologist called. The Oncotype test result was back; since I was over the line into the *high risk of recurrence* category, I needed to have chemo. Two days later, I had my hair cut and donated two 15-inch hanks of hair to Lovelocks. On February 21, I got a second opinion about treatment options and changed oncologists. The first one had left me with the uncomfortable feeling of having fallen through a crack some-where. On March 5, I'd have my first treatment; every week after that for 18-20 weeks, I'd have another. It turned out, on this every-week-treatment plan, I would not lose all my hair!

So, I would have more time than expected to learn all about Tucson and would experience the first half of a Tucson summer. I would keep painting and reading.

••• 26 •••
New Beginnings

Try not to resist the changes that come your way.
Instead let life live through you. — Rumi

REALIZING THAT A Tucson summer spent in an RV would be hell, I made an offer on a forty-year-old furnished double-wide and in April made the big move out of the apartment and into the mobile home (which I dubbed my *tin house*). It was in a lovely park in north Tucson, with a big heated pool and a spa. I was enjoying both.

Bijou developed what I hoped was a temporary anxiety disorder, due to the move into space almost triple the size of the apartment. Once I let her out of her carrier, she slunk down the hallway and hid under my bed for half a day. At last, she came out and, belly down almost to the floor, stealthily investigated the rooms and unfamiliar furnishings. She didn't like me out of her sight and voiced sad meows if I was. She was quiet and most happy if I was sitting in the big chair so she could be on my lap or tucked beside me, with a paw on my leg. She no longer slept curled up next to me at night; instead, she was busy trying out different chairs. There were so many choices.

Now I was in the throes of fixing things (the list was long), trying to organize my belongings in this space and get settled. I wanted to get back to the feeling of peacefulness, which had come over me suddenly in the past couple of months.

Little lizards scurried all over the place as I walked the Rillito Wash. There were whiptail lizards, zebra-tailed lizards which curl their black and white striped tail over their back like a scorpion as they dash across the path, and a biggish lizard with dark patches on his sides that I hadn't been able to identify. They were way too fast for me to get a photo.

I celebrated my 70th birthday in March and enjoyed the gift of a rainy day. Rain is always a cause for celebration in this dry state, so I greeted it with the proper amount of gratitude and enthusiasm.

One day, I got a ride down to the storage place and brought Mehitabel up to the storage area in the park.

I opened an account at a nearby credit union; little by little, I was becoming more official. Next, I needed to deal with inspections and re-registering the car and RV.

Dealing with cancer tends to focus your mind on now. What can I do now, at this moment? When you first get the news about an illness or when you suffer a loss of any kind, your mind is apt to run crazy with questions. Why me? Did I do something wrong? How did this happen? What will my life be like now? But, after a while, those thoughts settle down, and you must take it one step at a time, deal with it day by day.

⸺◦◦◦⸺

As of May 1, I was half-way through my course of 18 weekly chemo treatments. It wasn't the most enjoyable way to spend time, but the folks at Arizona Cancer Center were lovely. For the most part, the side effects had been minimal; food tasted odd, and I had some nausea, which I was able to control by drinking lots of water, tea, juice, or tonic water. I was more tired, though the move was responsible for much of that. If I could get through the second half of chemo as well as the first, I'd have no complaints.

Flowers were blooming everywhere. The nearby Tucson Mall had rows of palo verde trees covered with yellow flowers drifting everywhere in the breeze, turning the pavement to gold. The blossoms on the desert willow looked like miniature orchids; saguaros and other cacti were starting to bloom.

It was a lovely time of year to discover Tucson, though the temperatures were hard to take. They were regularly around 90, and a couple of days broke 100. In the RV, I'd be heading north this time of year, but I'd have to tough it out this summer.

The more I thought about it, the less I liked that phrase *in remission*. Cancer had struck twice, and I knew it could occur again, but right now, I didn't have cancer at all. It might never come back. But *in remission* sounded as though it was just asleep and could wake up at any moment. It was not as *gone* and wasn't as optimistic-sounding as I would like to feel.

I had no control over the fact that cancer had shown up in my life again. Both occurrences resulted in positive experiences, so I didn't feel sorry about them. I'd come full circle in a way, and Tucson was an excellent place to end up.

My original plan had been to take shorter trips with Bijou and Mehitabel during the summers. But somehow, I'd lost the momentum; the thought of loading and unloading the RV for a journey began to feel like a big deal. Plus, I was worrying some about money and thought I couldn't justify the cost of keeping Mehitabel now that I had the tin house. There were a few sleepless nights while deciding to sell, and part of me was devastated, knowing I'd miss the excitement of new vistas and new friends on the road. But I felt wonderfully at home here in Tucson, and I loved having the space to do art. I took Mehitabel to a dealer at the end of the summer. She'd given me some wonderful times over the past several years, but this was obviously another turning point. It was time to move on and decide what my plans were for this next period in my life.

At the end of September, I flew to North Carolina to visit my friend June and have the last of my worldly goods moved out of her attic, packed up, and shipped to Arizona.

The weather cooled down, and walks had taken the place of swimming for the time being. I joined a writers' group and continued with various art workshops.

Once I settled into my tin house, deciding it was time to dig in and deal with my stuffed fears and old beliefs, I dove into personal growth training in a big way through programs at Mindvalley.com. It worked. Between my meditation practice and the courses, the anger disappeared. I started recognizing the beliefs with which I'd been raised and understanding that many of them were no longer applicable. I never completely understood where the anger originated. Some was at my mother for not taking better care of herself, and some was at myself for not listening harder to my inner

GPS. But it was gone. I had a sense of peace, of being right where I belonged, doing work I loved.

So, another turning point; they do keep showing up. Every change means making adjustments. Some are hard, some relatively easy. I'd learned so much about myself since that first diagnosis of cancer: how to turn a challenge into an adventure, what I needed to feel happy and fulfilled, what I loved, how to set boundaries, and even how to ask for help. Also, how to change a tire, caulk a skylight, change the air filter on the generator, and repair a hose! Ending the RV adventure was hard, and sad; starting the new adventure here in Tucson was rewarding. I was so grateful that Bijou was with me; she was a loving and amusing companion.

I like change, learning new things, adventure, challenge, even when they initially scare me to death. When I feel stuck in a rut or a routine, I tend to push the boundaries, start something new, and always reach for the next big something.

Where will the future turning points lead me?

When we are no longer able to change a situation, we are challenged to change ourselves. —Viktor Frankl

Afterword

It's been eight years since I sold Mehitabel. I still miss the freedom she gave me to pick up and go. I sometimes think that I should get another RV and retire all over again to be a full-timer. Then I remember that I'm almost 78 and maybe that's not such a good idea. Unless I win the lottery, it's not possible anyway.

Am I afraid cancer will strike again? A little perhaps, but I'm doing my best to make that impossible. I had been careful of my health before, but I'm even more so now. It can be confusing sorting through various nutritional recommendations. Doctors and scientists have learned a lot over the past ten-twenty years. Most of it is the opposite of what the government told us for decades. I try to keep abreast of the new thinking and discoveries through my reading. I drink much less and stop altogether for a month or so a couple of times a year; I buy almost 100% organic groceries, eat very little meat, and stay away from factory-farmed meat and processed foods. I've continued my meditation practice.

Three years ago, I sold my tin house and bought a small condo up in the Foothills area north of the city. It's beautiful to see the mountains so close. I've visited Mexico twice and have thoughts of maybe moving there for good. I don't think I'm quite ready to make such a radical change, though. I'll have to give it a lot more thought.

Last April, I had to let Bijou go; her upper respiratory problems had gotten much worse, and I could see signs that the end was coming. It was heartbreaking to say goodbye to her.

The house felt way too empty after that, so in October 2019, I adopted a one-year-old Chihuahua/Jack Russell mix. I named him Squeaky. Initially, he had severe separation anxiety and would cry non-stop when I left to do errands, but he is gradually overcoming that and is a total delight, so bouncy. Watching him and his antics is a joy. I figured getting a dog this time would get me away from the computer and out walking several times a day. That thinking was sure right; three miles a day is the average. He is now the darling of my neighborhood and is making friends right and left.

I recently learned that I am a member of what is called *The Silent Generation*—those of us born between 1929 and 1945. I suddenly understood so much of my confusion during my relationship with Hal, as well as my marriages. We were the ones, especially the women, who were told to *suck it up, work hard, keep your head down and keep your mouth shut.* So, even though my internal GPS was telling me it wasn't going to work, my mind kept coming up with stories about how things would be better once this or that happened. I'm learning, slowly, to quiet my mind, pay more attention to my feelings, my intuition, and follow my internal GPS.

My dream now is to help women rediscover how strong and resourceful they are. We don't have to stay stuck in a job or a relationship that brings no joy. We can throw off that old programming. Step by step, it's possible to build a roadmap to a new life by following your internal GPS. You don't have to sell your house and everything you own as I did, but beware. Once you start dreaming about what might be possible, you never know what might happen.

Acknowledgments

A special thank you to friends who stepped forward to be my beta readers: Sue McAlary, Mikaela Quinn, Susan Wischmann, Judy Nakari. I so appreciate your eyes, your support, and your encouragement. An extra-special thank you to Laurie Pomeranz, my daughter-in-law, who insisted I unpack my emotions in this story. Her exact words, "You need to crack yourself open, girl!" And to Linda Cummings, who doesn't even like to read but read the entire manuscript, said she enjoyed it and kept asking, "But I want to know more about _____."

My editor, Traci Moore, was a perfect fit for me. She did just what I needed her to do, built up my confidence in things I did right and corrected me gently on things I could do better. She is blessed with keen eyes for mistakes and ears that are quick to hear words that seem out of tune.

A special shout-out goes to my writers' group, The Sonoran Scribes, for the countless times they patiently listened to me reading my travel journals, giving me valuable feedback and ideas. I've been part of this group of remarkable women for the past eight years, and they are a hugely important support to my writing spirit.

I am enormously grateful to all the helpful and inspiring people at Author Academy Elite: Kary Oberbrunner, Niccie Kliegl, Abigail Young, Nanette O'Neal, Daphne Smith, and many, many others.

About The Author

Susan Woodward was a Realtor® in Massachusetts and North Carolina for 23 years and had a sudden wake-up call at the age of 62. Faced with a diagnosis of breast cancer, she realized it was time to change course. She set her goals, made her plans, and three years later sold her house and almost everything she owned to become a full-time RVer, traveling North America with her cat Bijou for the next four-plus years.

Now settled in Tucson, Arizona, Susan writes, paints, and does personal coaching for women dealing with change and facing challenges. If you are struggling with a rough patch or feeling stuck in your job or relationship, the story of her decisions and what she learned about herself on her journeys is sure to inspire you.

In 2003, using her experience and knowledge of real estate, Susan co-authored *How to Make Your Realtor® Get You the Best Deal, NC Edition.*

Made in the USA
Coppell, TX
03 December 2020

42856050R00115